Real Estate Management Strategies & Tactics

How to Lead Agents and Managers to Peak Performance

Real Estate Management Strategies & Tactics

How to Lead Agents and Managers
to Peak Performance

Alain Pinel

BUSINESS
BOOKS

Winchester, UK
Washington, USA

JOHN HUNT PUBLISHING

First published by Business Books, 2020
Business Books is an imprint of John Hunt Publishing Ltd., No. 3 East St., Alresford,
Hampshire SO24 9EE, UK
office@jhpbooks.com
www.johnhuntpublishing.com
www.johnhuntpublishing.com/business-books

For distributor details and how to order please visit the 'Ordering' section on our website.

Text copyright: Alain Pinel 2020

ISBN: 978 1 78904 642 7
978 1 78904 643 4 (ebook)
Library of Congress Control Number: 2020935530

A CIP catalogue record for this book is available from the British Library.

Design: Stuart Davies

Printed and bound by CPI Group (UK) Ltd, Croydon, CR0 4YY

We operate a distinctive and ethical publishing philosophy in
all areas of our business, from our global network of authors to
production and worldwide distribution.

Contents

Contents

To the thousands of real estate sales managers out there whose job it is to perform miracles with a convincing smile and inspiring words of wisdom. They have two impatient bosses: upper-management or ownership full of expectations on one side and, on the other, independent agents/field soldiers who often think they are generals.

Introduction

I don't know how many kids, if any, actually dream of becoming Realtors when they grow up, but I was not one of them.

The hazards of life tricked me into a job I knew nothing about and had no interest in.

Having freshly landed here from a distant country (France) and coming from a vastly different line of work (journalism), selling real estate was not exactly natural, nor logical.

A real estate friend of mine, at the time, eventually succeeded in convincing me that this business was an enjoyable way to make a living. "You work when you want, as much or as little as you need depending on your golf commitments, you stay close to home, play with your kids, take a vacation from time to time and money is good." What's not to like?

Surprisingly enough, it worked out that way. Except that I worked my tail off, had to wait five years to go on a short vacation and never got a chance to play golf for the first twenty years.

At least I did well, professionally speaking. Sold a ton of real estate and stuffed my brain with anything and everything I could to be as good as I could be. It paid off.

One day, the president of the company offered me a "promotion," a management position in Saratoga, in the heart of what became known as the Silicon Valley.

I did not know any better. I said yes, not knowing then that my income would be slashed big time.

My office, a tiny pad and former pizza parlor sitting back from the main road and close to the railroad track was just fine and a juicy profit center for the company, thanks to the amazing eight associates I was lucky enough to inherit. I don't know who was managing who but we all had a blast.

The next office, up the street, was about ten times the size and quickly became the flagship of the company in the South Bay and a major money maker. I hired more associates than I can remember and coached plenty to master their craft.

Life was good. I loved my job. Never wanted to leave, but I did, to move to supposedly "better and bigger things," as we say.

Over the years, I got to wear many different hats in real estate management: office sales manager, vice president, regional manager, senior vice president, general sales manager, general manager, executive vice president, founder, owner, president, CEO, chairman.

The companies changed, every so many years. Some were big, some were huge, some were company-owned, some were part of a network; all leading companies in the country, in one category or another.

The horizons and battlegrounds changed as well: California, New England, Europe, Asia. Residential real estate (regional, national and international) remained my main livelihood interest but I often flirted with the commercial business as well as with new developments and investments.

I learned a lot along the way. Every day it seems like. The real estate business has sure changed tremendously since I got my license and it is changing even faster now, as if engulfed in a technology storm.

The funny thing is that, the more it changes, the more it stays the same. So to speak. After non-stop trials and tribulations, the industry seems to always revert back to "traditional" approaches. Agents, against all odds, are still at the center of all things real estate.

I don't think I have seen it all (still learning) but I have seen a lot and enjoyed the challenges along the exciting ride. Lots of friends who shared the ride with me pressed me to memorialize my success recipes. I did and here they are, in this book.

Managers, particularly those at the highest levels, need

information, raw unfiltered information. Knowledge is control. The proper/lucid/realistic use of such knowledge is power. Good decision-making takes emotion and subjectivity out of play.

That's what simple business methodology is all about: systems used as guides, quantitative and qualitative techniques, productivity analyses, graphic charts, stats expressed on "dashboards" of sort to force the obvious conclusions to jump off the screen so they can be properly addressed.

To make my job and that of my managers a bit easier and make success more predictable, measurable and sustainable, I created a bunch of such systems and "how to's." They cover most aspects of the business. They allowed me and others to avoid pitfalls and to understand at a quick glance the performance of any office, or region, or company.

Many of those planning or productivity tools are shown and demonstrated in this book. Some of them you may now use; some of them you may want to immediately put to good use.

Real estate is rarely predictable but your business should be.

The strategies and tactics I write about in this book have been and still are my guides to good business. They match my needs. You are welcome to make them yours and improve upon them so that they can match yours as well.

Chapter 1

Recruiting Agents

Recruiting sales associates is job #1 for a real estate manager.

Nothing - I mean, nothing - is more important. Why? Because agents are the ones who sell real estate and that's how we all make our living in the real estate industry.

That's where and how it all starts, and if the job is not done or not done well, that's where the story ends.

I don't care how smart and knowledgeable you may be and how good you think you are as an office sales manager, but if you cannot succeed at hiring sales associates, I doubt that you can succeed at all. You may consider going back to selling or look for another line of work.

If you are not sure whether to start looking for alternative career options, you can count on your regional/general manager or the EVP/president to soon let you know.

Recruiting agents is a never-ending process. You never have enough agents, especially if you don't have the right ones. You must always be looking for more and better ones.

A numbers game

I hate to admit it but, in a way, the more agents you have, the better, everything being equal.

You cannot win a battle in any marketplace with only a few soldiers, no matter how good. An office with a handful of knowledgeable and hardworking agents is usually no match for a large office reasonably well managed and filled with lots of agents, even if many of the agents are fairly new and inexperienced.

Real estate is a numbers game.

Generally speaking, the more associates you have, the more

visible your office is in the local market, the more prospecting activities you run, the more opportunities you have to connect with potential clients, the more SOI mailings/texts/tweets you send, the more open houses you hold over the weekend, the more buyers and sellers you get to meet, the more sales you put on the books, the more commission revenue you generate and the more money you end up making, as an office and as a company.

Again, it is a game of numbers and there is no short cut.

Who has a recruiting problem?

Just about every manager of any and all brokerage firms in your region, in the US and beyond. It is the nature of the business. We never have quite what we wish we had in the way of sales associates.

Some managers have a more concerning and perhaps urgent recruiting problem if:

- They have a hard time keeping agents
- They stand to lose 50% of their business if they lose 1 or 2 top producers
- They have in the office several agents that they would rather not have
- The competition is recruiting and they are not
- They have more desks than agents
- They are not making any money as an office
- The top agents are getting complacent or unreliable
- The bottom quartile is demoralized and going broke

Why is it so hard to recruit?

The answer(s) may be in the few following fundamentals:

- You can only attract agents if you are still capable of keeping happy and productive those you already have. Would they join your team today if they were not already with you?

- You need a solid and stable foundation. Hiring new agents, especially many of them over a short period of time, creates instability.

- You can only do well at the task if you can overcome the difficulties inherent to the growth process (tension, conflicts, etc.). Otherwise, you may not "digest" the newcomers well enough or fast enough. Ultimately, they will not feel welcome, they will fail and they will quit and, in the process, so will many demoralized good producers.

- Also, you can attract new agents only if you are different, as an organization, as an office, as a manager... from the company, the office and the manager that the prospects are considering leaving.

That's why it is so important to ask potential recruits, early in a recruiting interview, what they don't like (if anything) about their existing office. Is their dissatisfaction due to the company, or the manager, or some fellow associates?

Their answers will pretty much tell you what they are looking for. Only then will you know what they need and therefore what you need to say.

Once you understand their motivations, the timing is prime to ask what they know and how they feel about your office and/or your company. They probably think it is a good office/company or, at least, they are somewhat intrigued and curious about you. If not, chances are they would not take the time to meet with you in the first place.

The more they will share about any good feeling they have about you and your brand, the more comfortable they will feel about the idea of moving, the more they will picture themselves in the "uniform" and the more committed they progressively will be to join your team.

- Another fundamental to keep in mind - somewhat related to the previous point, is that experienced agents considering a move are generally unhappy where they are, for whatever reason. So, if you want them, it stands to reason that you should try to make them feel comfortable. A question like "do you now have a happy office?" would be a smart one to ask.

- Obviously, you must know what is so good and compelling about your company, what makes you different, better, stronger. Keeping in mind what it is they need and want, you could talk about vision, leadership, agents' services, marketing programs, technology, financial stability, "partnership" with the agents, a clear vision for our growth, one-stop shopping concept with strong mortgage and insurance arms, outstanding full time professionals in the business... Whatever is appropriate.

Make a mental list of what you recognize as the brand or the office key differentiators that give you an edge over the competition, to score big if and when prospects complain about the lack of one or more of such benefits at their present brokerage.

Be careful not to talk too much and oversell. Questions are often the best answers.

Attitude

Potential recruits are like home buyers: they would like to "buy" a company or an office... But they may not. As "buyers," they are emotional, even if they ask rational questions. A good experienced manager knows what to ask and when.

Questions about commission splits and such may not be as important as you think. More often than not, candidates are looking for more recognition, more opportunities for success. They want to be happy, comfortable, and proud of their association. Your attitude is key to creating the right ambiance:

- As a manager, you must appear enthusiastic and happy to be where you are. You must create an atmosphere of relaxation that may allow the potential recruit to open up and actually enjoy the meeting.
- When interviewing experienced agents, avoid harassing them with "red tape" questions like goals and objectives. At this stage of the game it does not mean a thing. Keep the atmosphere warm and friendly. Numbers come last, not first.
- You must have an optimistic attitude about the business, the market, the company, etc. So should they. If they have a negative attitude and are down on the market, or the business, or the company, you may very well be wasting your time.

Applicants need to be wanted. They need to know that the office they consider joining is full of terrific people who are looking forward to welcoming them and working with them.

The support system, from the agents, the staff, and the company as a whole, is absolutely critical. As managers, you have to provide the conditions for such support and "sell" it to the prospects.

Consideration, recognition, and support from everyone in the office/company are legitimate concerns of new agents. If you make them your concerns as well, you are offering newcomers what they are looking for.

New agents vs. experienced agents

Generally speaking, good seasoned agents are the top recruiting choice. That's a no brainer. However, experienced vs. new is often the wrong issue, or the right issue taken out of context. Most of the time, the dilemma is not "who should you hire" but "who can you hire." It is often a question of maturity and, when in doubt, the answer is quite simply "get who you can."

I do not mean to be facetious but an agent is at least as good as a "For sale" sign, and you need many of those planted in front lawns to be perceived as a real player in the local market. If you need more associates and a new licensee shows desire, potential, and has a reasonably good business brain, hire!

If he/she seems to be at least as good as the worst agent in your office, give the newbie a chance. Get him/her to commit to a strict schedule of prescribed activities and report back to you regularly. That's the beginning of coaching.

Be sure to focus on the agents who best fit your needs, in terms of dedication, drive, image, objectives, prospecting, marketing, and commitments to activities such as open houses. It is a big plus if they reside in the local market.

To test the new licensees' sense of purpose, it is a good idea to ask the following question: "If you do not succeed in this business, what will you do? Do you have something else to fall back on?"

If they start talking about Plan B, they implicitly admit they very well might fail and then, there is a good chance they will. Probe for more information before you decide whether you still want to bother.

The "I only want experienced agents" statement can make sense, in theory at least, but it could merely be an excuse to cover up a recruiting problem. If you need agents, there is nothing wrong with new people. As a matter of fact, the infusion of new blood, new spirit, new energy is refreshing, challenging, and badly needed sometimes in established offices that are a bit stuffy and full of seasoned associates growing old.

If the office is "full" (again, it never is) and you are satisfied with everyone (you never are), and you have a "waiting list," then I kind of agree that preference should be given to successful agents. It's a no brainer. They bring with them their reputation, their book of past and existing clients, and whatever business they have in the pipeline.

There is a time for everything though. If the office is half empty and crying for help, it is foolish to wait for superstars.

Start at the beginning: fill up the office. Then, fine tune and upgrade, one person at a time. When the office is fully occupied, it will undoubtedly be busier and more attractive to potential experienced agents.

That's the process. You cannot start with step 2; you have to start with step 1.

Shopping tips to recruit experienced agents

- Be a visible manager
- Make it a habit of going regularly on the weekly regional MLS tour of new listings to shake hands and exchange a few friendly words with the agents you ideally would love to see in your office
- Great idea to say hi and visit when they are holding an open house
- If and when seeing them in their office, offer a big friendly smile
- Send them a "Thank you" note when they are involved in a co-broke transaction
- Congratulate them on their specific achievements/awards. When their impressive production numbers are known for the entire year, be sure to send them a personal handwritten letter
- When they stop by your office for business purposes, make them feel welcome and greet them personally
- Invite them to office parties and, when appropriate, to recognition meetings and training seminars
- Send them samples of documents/tools your company is successfully using when you know they would love their broker to offer the same
- Subscribe them, whenever appropriate, to your newsletter or blogs

- Make them feel as if they were already part of the team
- Make sure the key agents in your office are on your side and play your game. They may be the best recruiters.

Team recruiting exercise

Invite a select group of 4-5 key established and respected agents to play an effective role in the recruiting process. They will always be happy to help if you present the invitation as a mark of your esteem and your trust in their good judgment.

It could go as follows:

"You are the finest professionals. I wish I had more agents like you, agents we can all benefit from, agents who can make us even stronger as an office."

"Come to think of it, let me ask you: out of all the good and experienced agents in town, who would you actually like to see in our office –agents who share your ethics, your values? Think of one or two."

"Perhaps you can tell them that I will be calling them on your recommendation, and I will make it my job to hire them, for your benefit and that of the entire office."

There are many ways to incite key agents to help you with the recruiting and reward them for doing it successfully.

Business routine

Hiring is a matter of ordinary business routine. It is both a survival requirement in a competitive and predatory market and the key to top performance.

Remember: there is no such thing as a full office.

Remember also to have fun recruiting. The process can be as enjoyable as the rewards. Don't forget to smile.

Chapter 2

Retaining Agents

It's one thing to recruit agents, it's another to keep them. I don't really know which one of the two tasks is more complicated, except to say that you don't have to worry about retention if you don't hire people to begin with.

I guess that's one way to say that hiring is job #1 and must always be the manager's top of mind.

At least, if you already have existing agents in the office, it's easier to get more of the same. The office is alive with real agents and open for business. Over time, both quantity and hopefully quality will logically improve in the right environment.

Now, the challenge is to keep your existing agents happy and productive.

Happy agents are usually productive and loyal to you and the company. But don't count on it. You may be good but you are not the only office in town. Other brokers are awfully busy trying to seduce and lure your good agents with sugary promises of a better split, recruiting bonuses, private offices, a marketing budget or more tools, more personal attention, more coaching, etc. Invitations and promises are flying non-stop, 24/7.

To keep agents, the best advice is to keep your eyes and your ears open. Before the fire, there is smoke. Agents leave for a reason and there are signs that you could see, hear, or feel that suggest that something no good is brewing.

The news about an agent leaving (or a group of agents as it is often the case) should never be a surprise. In other words, the bad news can be avoided if detected and dealt with early.

Red flags/Indicators

Here are some of the signs or events that smell trouble:

- The agent does not come to the office
- No show at the weekly sales meeting
- No participation at office/company workshops or meetings
- If and when in the office, does not interact with other agents
- Expresses negativity and complains when in a conversation with others
- Meeting in dark corners with other negative associates
- Avoids the manager
- Moving boxes
- Downloading personal or office files
- Personal production way down
- No open house activity
- Does not use company programs or services
- Has not paid MLS or Board dues
- Has not paid his/her E&O
- No more listings on the books
- No more pending sales
- Split rollback on the horizon
- Rumors

Risk prevention

What can you do to prevent an exodus?

Somehow, you need to create an alarm system that will alert you about the possible danger before it strikes. Such alarm systems can be created in concert with many of the people who surround you: the administrative staff, IT and marketing coordinators, the ancillary services representatives who call regularly on the agents, even title/escrow companies, mortgage people, and inspection outfits reps who visit your office to solicit business.

Generally speaking, you will likely smell trouble if you stay close to your agents. There are so many ways to do this. Pick and choose, or do them all:

- "Work the aisles" everyday
- Show care, concern, appreciation
- "What can I do to help?"
- Smile
- One-on-one business plan meetings at least twice a year
- One-on-one (monthly?) monitoring meetings to keep agents on track
- Socials/wine & cheese
- Offer to assist with mailings
- Provide personal coaching or suggest training
- Send them a Thank you note when they get a listing or a sale
- Congratulate them on their specific achievements/awards
- Be visible in the office

Manager's Profile

In his/her office, the manager is the company. As such, you have to shine all the time. There is no bad day; there is no bad time. You must be a source of support, inspiration, motivation to keep on charging the agents' battery.

You accomplish the above with two basic things: a brain and a smile. One of the two is not enough, both are required.

We've seen elsewhere (see "recruiting agents" chapter) that you can successfully recruit newcomers only to the extent that the foundation of existing agents is stable and happy. Let's spend a little time on the subject.

What are the most common criticisms we hear from associates with respect to their manager?

- He/she is "never" in the office
- He/she is not listening or attending to our needs
- He/she is arrogant and does not sincerely care about us
- When in the office, he/she is behind closed doors talking to people who have nothing to do with the office...

- He/she is not fair

Perception or reality? Same thing here. Remember that you are "managers" only if: 1) You have agents to...manage, 2) the agents want to be managed by...you. Otherwise you may be many things but you are not managers.

If you want agents to be content, stimulated, proud, and loyal so that they may go to bat and try to recruit for you (ideal situation), you have to make them feel as your true partners or customers.

Interestingly enough, the more attentive and considerate you are or appear to be, the happier the agents are and the less they seem to need your time. Otherwise, just for the sake of attention and recognition, they will demand to see you, even for no good reason. See some smoke?

Don't miss the signal. If you do, they will feel abandoned; a part of them will already be out the door.

Limits

Of course, trying to make people happy has got to stop somewhere. You certainly should never do it blindly. Let's not give away smiles and candies to people who are sinking the ship. If you do, you may encourage apathy and failure for the sake of happiness.

When opening and growing a new/newer office (particularly a large one), with the responsibility of hiring fast and furious, you depend a great deal on the cooperation of the agents who are already there. In such scenario, a manager typically goes through 2 different phases:

- First, make your "junior team" happy in spite of performance numbers that may not justify pats on the back. In fact, in many cases, the stats will stink. That's the stabilization mode, the honeymoon phase. Be cautious not to prolong this period too long as to avoid falling in the trap of rewarding mediocrity. If they are failing, "happy" people are not welcome. Sorry.

- As soon as possible in the building process, establish and communicate guidelines/standards for individual success so that agents have a measuring stick to judge their performance and become more accountable. It is your job to hold them to those standards. If you don't, you don't need standards.

What to do when bad happens

Again, there should not be a surprise when agents pack their bags since the "presumption of guilt" is almost always there to be seen if you care enough to look.

Nevertheless, sometimes bad happens, and when it does, it may not be too late to change the outcome if you act quickly, decisively, and adequately. For example:

- Have an urgent friendly face to face meeting with the agent you don't want to lose
- Let your heart speak: you are "surprised," you are hurt
- Probe for information: why?
- Isolate the reasons/issues and try to cure them, one at a time
- Find out where the agent plans on going and when
- Attempt to resell them on the office and the company. If they don't know the benefits of association, no wonder they are curious to know if the grass is greener elsewhere
- If appropriate, use other key and loyal agents (the family) to assist you in trying to dissuade the agent from leaving
- Solicit the support of the administrative staff if they are not part of the problem
- "What can I do (or what can the company do) to change your mind?"

- Involve senior management ASAP
- Involve HR if and when relevant
- Keep your fingers crossed...

Chapter 3

Self-assessment

We, human beings, don't mind judging others, but when asked to assess our own strengths and weaknesses, the answers are hard to find. Is that for excess of humility or for lack of a point of reference? Both?

Regardless what it is, we are not good and comfortable with the exercise. Yet it can prove to be a valuable one for managers to appraise the skills and the character of an agent and/or for upper management to evaluate the abilities, competences, and the character of an office sales manager.

In both cases, a self-assessment questionnaire should be used when hiring a new agent (brand new or one moving from a competitor) or a new manager (same idea).

1 - New agents

Objectives of the self-assessment questionnaire:

- Allow the new associates to try to identify their own aptitudes, competences, talents, skills, as well as their challenges and weaknesses
- Allow the hiring manager to identify the difference between the new agents' perception of their strong or weak points and the reality, in order to help them better leverage their skills and maximize their performance. (See agent's questionnaire)

As you can see on the form, the list is rather exhaustive. Most activities an agent can engage in are listed. As a manager, you may want to finetune the list, add or delete those activities which may not be relevant to your needs or in your particular market.

In most cases, the answers an agent provides are pretty close to what you will indeed be able to observe and verify. They usually know what they are good at and what they are not good at. Sometimes, however, they are off big time.

In my manager's years, I met hundreds of associates who were intent on believing that they mastered such skills as listing presentation or open house hosting, when in fact they sometimes were mediocre at one or both tasks.

They just wanted to believe that they were good because they recognized that these activities were critically important to you and the company. They confused the value of the activities and their aptitude at performing them.

As a coach, you need to make sure they can see themselves as they are and help them better exploit their knowledge and their skills, whatever they may be.

Help agents get better at what they are good at

Two things to keep in mind: 1) nobody is good at everything, 2) you only have so much time to spend coaching an agent.

If you feel that your time is well spent and will soon be rewarded helping a weak agent become great at developing a mailing campaign, go ahead and do it. It's your time and it's your profit center. If, however, you find that the agent is a natural at successfully leveraging open houses or marketing himself/herself to potential clients, make your and the agent's job easy: get the agent to leverage those skills as much as possible and as soon as possible for the commission dollars to start coming sooner than later.

In my experience, I can guarantee that it is way smarter to help agents get better at what they are already good at than try, against all odds, to teach them how to become good at what they don't like or what they are lousy at doing.

If you allow me a so-so analogy, it does not do anybody any good to encourage a left-handed person to write with the right hand.

All agents are human beings (I think). As such, they are all different, with unique competences and talents that we, as managers, want to further develop. If we are not capable of doing it well, it is part of our job to refer individual agents to an in-house coach/trainer or an outside coach/guru.

If we want to keep the agent, he/she might as well learn, somehow, how to make money for the company.

Self assessment questionnaire – Agents

Please give yourself a grade, from 1 to 5 (5 being the best) in the following fields of competence and performance:

Open house activity   1 2 3 4 5
Geographic farming   1 2 3 4 5
Mailings (brochures, newsletters, new
  listings, etc.)   1 2 3 4 5
Prospecting via email, texts, tweets   1 2 3 4 5
Telephone – cold calling   1 2 3 4 5
Social media   1 2 3 4 5
Marketing/Advertising   1 2 3 4 5
Listing presentations   1 2 3 4 5
Closing a sale   1 2 3 4 5
Sale/closing follow up   1 2 3 4 5
Clients' parties   1 2 3 4 5
Technology savvy   1 2 3 4 5
Knowledge of contracts and other transaction
  forms   1 2 3 4 5
Knowledge of the transaction process   1 2 3 4 5
Knowledge of the real estate business   1 2 3 4 5
Knowledge of the local market   1 2 3 4 5
Legal and tax aspects of the business   1 2 3 4 5
Company programs, services and policies   1 2 3 4 5
Ethics   1 2 3 4 5

Value of customer service	1 2 3 4 5
Team player	1 2 3 4 5
Positive attitude	1 2 3 4 5
Availability	1 2 3 4 5
Determination	1 2 3 4 5
Presentation	1 2 3 4 5
Networking	1 2 3 4 5

2 - New managers

Much of what we said above regarding agents applies for managers as well.

The objectives are similar:

- Allow the office sales managers to identify their aptitudes, competences, talents, skills, as well as their challenges and weaknesses
- Allow upper-management (regional/general manager/ EVP/president/...) to identify the difference between the managers perception of their strong or weak points and the reality, in order to help them focus on priorities, better leverage their skills and help maximize the performance of the office.

(See manager's questionnaire)

I found the questionnaire to be very important to understand and appreciate the managers' versatility. A manager needs to wear many different hats and needs to be comfortable and effective with most of the various daily, weekly, monthly, and annual tasks/responsibilities, for the benefit of the office and the benefit of the company.

It is not uncommon for managers to brag and exaggerate somewhat their skills and proficiencies. Not a good idea though. Better to show a bit of humility when filling out the questionnaire because actual performance numbers and financial stats don't lie; they largely reflect the effectiveness of the managers as well as the wellbeing of the offices they are responsible for.

Results are results and, unless the manager has no latitude on strategic choices nor control over the means to achieve expected objectives, the manager has to assume both the ownership and the consequences of his/her decisions.

This self-assessment document can prove to be very helpful to upper-management when evaluating managers. Has the manager what it takes to run a particular office, in a particular market? Has the manager a clear vision of his/her own capabilities such that he/she can optimize personal strengths and correct any eventual deficiency?

Key indicators/red flags

- Result oriented and profit driven: the last line (bottom line) of a financial report is what business is all about and, accordingly, the manager must be good at the sport and remain focused on the objectives. At the end of the day, that's what the manager is going to be judged on. If the results are not what they should be, it's up to upper-management to review the manager's weaknesses, check those which can be remedied and define specific action steps to correct the situation
- Recruiting: Job #1. If well done, recruiting has a way to correct most actual or potential problems
- Staff: never underestimate the immense power and value of an administrative assistant or a marketing/IT coordinator. They have the agents' ears and often are the go-to persons for failing or unhappy associates. The managers' right arms, their conscience, and their number one support system. Treat with TLC
- Leadership: are the agents fighting for the manager and follow his/her vision, decisions, choices? (See management vs. leadership chapter)

- Technology: whether we like it or not, it is driving the business. Better be savvy enough to use efficiently and inspirational enough to get the agents to use 24/7 in their prospecting, marketing, networking, planning, record keeping, etc.
- Training: on-going. The business keeps on changing. We all need to learn and adapt to remain relevant and have a chance to improve
- Cooperation: no matter how good we are as an office and/ or a company, we largely depend on other companies and agents to feed us with their listings and sell ours. It pays to be nice to the competition
- Customer service: should go without saying. We work for the clients, whether buyers or sellers. We cannot work without them. They are the ones who pay us
- Availability: you may be knowledgeable as a manager but if you are not around the office or easily reachable when agents need you, you will not be the manager very long
- Planning: do you know what you want to achieve and how to get there? Say yes.

Self-assessment questionnaire – Managers

Please give yourself a grade, from 1 to 5 (5 being the best) in the following fields of expertise and performance:

Recruiting	1 2 3 4 5
Retention	1 2 3 4 5
Management skills	1 2 3 4 5
Coaching	1 2 3 4 5
Training	1 2 3 4 5
Leadership	1 2 3 4 5
Business acumen	1 2 3 4 5
Customer service	1 2 3 4 5
Ethics	1 2 3 4 5

Real estate knowledge	1 2 3 4 5
Financials	1 2 3 4 5
Business planning	1 2 3 4 5
Marketing	1 2 3 4 5
Technology	1 2 3 4 5
Social media	1 2 3 4 5
Knowledge of the company programs and services	1 2 3 4 5
Administrative matters	1 2 3 4 5
Knowledge of the company procedures and policies	1 2 3 4 5
Legal questions	1 2 3 4 5
Tax aspects of the business	1 2 3 4 5
People's skills	1 2 3 4 5
Team work	1 2 3 4 5
Community involvement	1 2 3 4 5
Knowledge of the market	1 2 3 4 5
Time management	1 2 3 4 5
Availability	1 2 3 4 5

Chapter 4

Agents' Quartiles

What kind of agents do you want?

What kind of agents do you need?

What kind of agents can you get?

Questions...Questions... Always the same, regardless of the marketplace, the company and the manager in charge of recruiting.

No office managers, of any company, anywhere, can say they have the ideal agents' makeup. The right number, the right profiles, the right chemistry. There is always a good reason, if not a need to do better. It's a never-ending quest.

Agents come and go, for a multitude of reasons.

Good agents can move out of the area, or turn complacent, or burnout and start faltering.

Many weak or brand-new agents may not last enough to give themselves (and you) a chance to succeed, although some will with time and proper nurturing.

It takes all kinds.

Managers usually have a recruiting plan, based on what they perceive their needs to be or what they are told to do by upper management. But let's face it, for the most part, they hire who they can when it looks like a reasonably good risk. Hiring associates is a process made of opportunities.

Who would you hire, given the choice?

Brand-new agents: OK, why not? There are many in any given pond and they are a lot easier to sign than well-known seasoned professionals. They have what appears like an advantage: they start (or should) at the bottom of the commission schedule, in other words they pay the House a large chunk of the gross commission. When they sell that is, and that's the problem. It might take months for them to produce their first transaction and months again to enter a second one on the books.

Meanwhile they consume a lot of your time and that of your staff, training directors and IT people. You may end up spending more than what you could ever expect in return for your investment. Also, they may cause conflicts with some existing good agents who may ponder staying in an office that caters to new associates.

If and when the newbies make it, it is kind of nice. It is largely because of you, the manager and what the company has to offer in the way of services.

You hired them, you groomed them and you turned them into home grown pros. They like you. They feel like they "owe" you. They are loyal to you, at least for a while. They become proud "company people" and could help you recruit other associates because they like to sell their success story and you are part of it.

Top producers: that's a no brainer: if you can get top producers to join you and your team, go for it at full speed.

Yes, they may cost you plenty as a commission split, but they list and sell so much that you love to enjoy the pain when you see the gold.

Besides, for the first few months, you "pay" them with their own money... the money that will result from their transferred pending transactions (if allowed), the money that will result from negotiating with existing clients and the money that will flow sooner or later from the sale of existing (if allowed) or upcoming listings.

One little damper though to temper your hiring enthusiasm: some top producers may not be welcome in your office. I am talking especially about temperamental prima donnas who may disturb the peace and stability of your team members. Be vigilant when hiring and keep your eyes open for a while after you do.

The hunt for top producers is so wild that many companies

do not hesitate to "buy" some with phenomenal six figures recruiting bonuses, or upfront marketing dollars, or whatever shines and can persuade them to sign.

Do I like these tactics? No, I positively hate funny-smelling tactics that can tarnish the reputation of Realtors.

To me, they show more weakness than strength. But they work! Whether I/we like them or not, they work.

"Middle producers": anybody in between the two above mentioned categories.

Quartiles guidelines

I remember well a roundtable session I co-organized a few years ago on the subject matter. My managers had to think out loud about the four main categories of agents, offer specific profile guidelines for each one and exchange ideas on how to best leverage the dynamics of the various groups.

(See the "Office quartile analysis")

The quartiles analysis, as shown on the table, can differ somewhat from one office to another, depending for example on such factors as the reputation of the company and the quality of the manager.

The percentages attributed to each agents' category will vary but, overall, the findings and conclusions are fairly consistent throughout the profession.

Group A – *Dominant segment: top producers*
Profile: winners, type A players, self-motivated, mostly independent. They use the company strengths but add their own tools/marketing to differentiate themselves and grow their own brand, often with team members.

- % of the office roster: 10%
- % of recommended manager's time: 15 to 35%

OFFICE QUARTILES ANALYSIS

GROUP A

Category	Top Producers
Management Time (guideline)	20%
Traits	Need Recognition (lunch, etc)
	Problem Solving
	Senior Management Relationship
	Proactive on Building Relationship
	Get Involved with Sales Meetings

GROUP B

Category	Core Producers
Management Time (guideline)	40%
Traits	Coaching / Training
	Business Planning
	Marketing Systems
	Frequent Meetings
	Training / Webinars

GROUP C

Category	Need Help
Management Time (guideline)	35%
Traits	Accountability
	Training
	Coaching
	Manager Tells Them To Do List
	Prospecting

GROUP D

Category	Leave Alone
Management Time (guideline)	5%
Traits	Giving up or gave up already

Opportunities: since they are the biggest money makers in the office, they need to be treated as such. If and when they are, they often have a positive influence on the rest of the team and offer great assistance with the recruiting.

To a large extent, they are the office: its identity, its image and its financial picture.

It should be noted that even though they contribute a lot to the office production and bottom line, it is generally easier to get them to improve and increase their business than it is to expect B players to increase their production.

The huge manager's time allocation mentioned above (between 15% and 35%) is a function of many variables: the agents themselves (all top producers are unique in the way they work and place different demand on the manager's time) and also the style of management.

Is it better to leave the A players alone? Or keep close and multiply the opportunities to interact with them? Well, don't worry too much about this, they will let you know. Trust me. If they need your time, attention, advice, help, they will get it. If and when they don't, there is trouble.

Threats: to repeat what was just said, A players need attention, even if they don't need you. Beware. They are the franchise players. They are wanted and are continually solicited by competitors.

They can leave from one day to the next if they don't get what they need from you and the company. When they do, here goes a large fraction of the office production, profit, reputation, attractiveness and overall stability.

Group B – *Dominant segment: core producers*
Profile: bread and butter players, backbone of the office, seasoned producers, usually set in their ways, satisfied somewhat of their production, loyal to the office/company and proud of their association.

- % of the office roster: 50%
- % of recommended manager's time: 35 to 40%

Opportunities: since they are the foundation of the office, they are a barometer of sort of the office stability and success.

The more you help them, the more they want to please, and the better the overall performance of the office. They are your partners. Hence trying to consistently rally them behind company programs, even if they resist at first. It is the best way (only way?) for some of them to eventually move up to the A Team.

Excellent reservoir of field trainers as they offer both knowledge and loyalty.

Threats: They expect recognition from the manager. Morale issues may arise if the manager is avaricious of his/her time and attention. If one B agent is unhappy, the contagion spreads quickly. Watch activities and body language. Be aware of those who no longer come to the weekly sales meeting or those who are slowing down with mailings and open houses.

Needs: B associates need hands-on teaching of technology tools, company programs and help with company advertising as they usually do little if anything on their own. They look up to you as a manager and need regular stroking from you. They need a clear vision of the company identity and business model.

Group C – *Dominant segment: new/newer agents*
Profile: Newer recruits, whether new licensees or transfers from another brokerage. Eager to learn, execute and hopefully succeed. Happy to use technology to facilitate their work and grow their sphere of influence. Avid consumers of information, training, coaching, techniques, tips.

- % of the office roster: 30%
- % of the recommended manager's time: 35 to 40%

Opportunities: Huge. The C group is the future of the office/ company. It's money in the bank if properly nurtured. If you willing and able to take good care of them, the ambitious in the group will soon join the A Team.

Threats: the other side of the medal... If you cannot cater to their real needs, chances are they will fail and every minute you invested with them will have been nothing but a waste of time. Some will quit the business altogether, some will join a different company and some will drop quickly to the D group and die slowly but surely.

Group C mortality rate is exceptionally high, but so are the possible rewards. This group has the largest growth potential. It represents one of your biggest challenges: how can you bring newer agents up to speed and regularly improve their performance and their productivity?

One way this can be done is to implement a field training program where they can shadow and assist a seasoned agent. Not to mention enrolling the newbie in all kinds of training classes and workshops.

Needs: direction from the manager, right from the start. As soon as the agent joins, you develop a tailor-made business and marketing plan with the agent. What he/she should do during the first thirty days is most important to set the tone and establish accountability.

All prescribed measurable activities, such as open house, creating a SOI list, planning a direct mail program, etc. are a must do, and so is a commitment to attend training in every discipline, as recommended by the manager

To be fully meaningful and effective, the first thirty-day to-do list has to be reviewed and monitored every week (if not more often) by the manager. Tough but necessary.

Group D – *Dominant segment: does not really matter!*
Profile: Agents who are giving up or gave up a long time ago.

- % of the office roster: 10%
- % of recommended manager's time: 0 to 5%

In conclusion, one piece of advice: put the time where the money is.

Chapter 5

Space Accommodations

I do not doubt that all real estate agents are born equal, but they sure evolve at different speed and in many different ways through their professional years.

Some are good, some not so much. Among the good ones, some are amazing. They are the franchise players. They pretty much get what they want, including choice space within the office.

There is only so much space in an office and what to do with it, how to best leverage it, largely depends on the company business model.

Back many-many moons ago, it was considered normal to have a desk for each agent, good or bad, experienced or new. As unbelievable as it may seem, it was not all that uncommon for some so-called managers to say "my office is full, I can't hire, I don't have a free desk."

So much for the distant past. We have known for a long time that there is not necessarily any correlation between space and the number of associates.

Depending on the market and the business model, it's OK to have an office with 10 desks or so and 150 agents.

In fact, who says you need desks in the first place? A conference room or two might suffice.

Do not read in this statement that I agree with the above concept. I don't. I don't care at all for body shops or ghost offices where agents only work offsite. But force is to recognize that these options exist. It takes all kinds.

Workstations

Between a plethora of desks and no desks at all, there is a

multitude of options and plenty of variations to each one. Workstations is one of the options. It has been quite popular and still is.

A simple long and narrow counter/desk can do the job and accommodate lots of come-and-go agents. All they need is room for their laptop or tablet and, just in case, a couple of plugs and phone jacks.

The café-type variation, with ample counter space and a few bar stools, is an appealing and fashionable concept. It is welcoming to both agents on the move and clients.

Workstations can accommodate any number of people and are particularly pertinent - if not attractive - for new people whose primary objective is to be with you/the office/the company, no matter where.

Most of their time has to be spent in the field anyway, previewing property, prospecting, and learning the market. If and when they expect clients, they are welcome to use a conference room.

The concept is excellent but it will only work (read: you will only make it work) if you are sold on it, otherwise, you will not be very convincing at trying to sell it... And the workstation will soon become another shelf for another pile of papers.

In time, when one "workstation agent" starts flourishing and performs better than a "desk-agent," it will be a clear signal that a switch should take place. Agent A earned a desk while agent B no longer deserves one. This is a competitive job. Space does not belong to the agents, but they still have to earn it.

Desk sharing

Here again, the concept can only work if you believe in it. It must be introduced as a way of life and a "plus" for the office as a whole.

The idea is simple. It sounds like a job definition: it is your responsibility, as a manager, to maximize the profitability of each and every desk. That's why managers spend time, at the regional or company meetings, working on the EDO (Effective Desk Occupancy) and look at each desk as an individual profit center.

To arrive at the expected result, a manager may demonstrate that the best system is "1 agent/1 desk" or find that a "floating desk" will better serve his/her needs, or again that "desk sharing" has the advantage of increasing the office population and creates incremental business without significant overhead increase.

Hard sale? Maybe, maybe not; it's all in the mind. After all, agents want to associate with the best office, and the best office is usually the hardest one to join and stay with.

Existing agents should be proud of the fact that their office is wanted and the seats are hard to get. There is a price to pay to belong.

As in the case of workstations, desk sharing is often a temporary condition predicated on performance. Occupants can move up or move out.

Private offices

If, as a manager, you like challenges and you don't mind having a chronic headache, you will love having to deal with private offices.

Give a larger cubicle or a private office to an agent and you just created a prima donna.

Of course, if you have private offices and if you choose not to give one to an emerging prima donna in recognition for the volume of business he/she brings to the cash register, you may soon lose the prima donna to the competition.

(Decisions, decisions. Do you really want to be a manager?)

There are "private offices" and there are "private offices." Don't be confused.

Some are bigger than others.

Some are small, say for two or three people, some are big

enough for about five, and some are huge and can accommodate a mega team... An office within an office.

With only rare exceptions, the bigger the office and the less control you can exercise over the occupants, particularly when the major occupant is a strong team leader whose production represents a huge fraction of the office production/revenue.

Who is managing who? The "laissez faire"-type manager does not mind too much, unless and until the top producer, who is left alone for fear of making waves, decides to leave and causes the office to quickly switch from profit to loss and may have to close its doors.

Office for rent

In the real estate universe, business models are too many to count and too complex to even understand.

Lots of companies, big or small, choose to offer space, a marketing name/brand and a number of tools and services for big ego agents who love to play solo and do not care to have a so-called manager babysitting them.

In that case, the option of paying the office a rental fee for space in exchange for a higher split may be a good formula. The company receives a regular rental income that reduces overhead/ risks and the agent writes off the expense. Looks like a win-win.

"Home office"

For decades now, real estate companies have been playing with the pros and cons of having brick and mortar offices.

Back in the old days, the question was not yet a valid question: a well identified physical plant with a company name/logo on the façade was a must.

Over the years, with operating expenses going up and the House share of the commission income going down, some brokerages got the idea that some agents are better off working offsite if that's what they wish.

More and more independent top producers prefer to open shop in an office separate from that of the company as such, although the resulting "satellite office" or quasi franchise of sort needs to display the name of the company (and usually bears also the name of the agent's own brand).

This formula is a way for a company to keep the agent in the fold rather than losing him/her altogether. In that case, the company picks up the tab on many of the standard business expenses (utilities and perhaps a fraction of the rent) and may give the agent a better split.

Chapter 6

Effective Desk Occupancy – EDO

As a manager, you are not required to provide a desk to each one of your associates but if you do, you might as well get them to pay for it, in one way or another. Makes sense? Say yes.

I happen to like an approach that attributes to an agent a prorated office overhead cost on the basis of desk space, even if it is somewhat arbitrary. At least it is simple enough to prove a point: whether or not an agent produces a lot of revenue for the benefit of the office, he/she contributes to the overhead.

That's what the "Effective Desk Occupancy" study is about. That's its value. It is a constant reminder for managers to read their P & L and try to maximize the return on brick and mortar investment and operating expenses. It is largely used by real estate brokerages throughout the country and beyond to evaluate the financial well-being of an office and its potential growth.

Like any approach to office cost analysis, the EDO is not perfect since there are so many different and conflicting business models in play in our industry. We must recognize that offices have multiple personalities and come in all shapes:

- Some offices provide a desk to every associate
- Some offices get all or a fraction of the agents to share desks, whether based on revenue, or newness, or time in the office, or whatever
- Some offices have no agents' desks
- Some offices provide top agents with private offices which may be five or ten times the standard "desk space"
- Some offices are virtual, with no physical presence. The agents work offsite

Keeping in mind the above contingencies, let's see how the Effective Desk Occupancy study works and how it can help you better understand what each one of your agents brings to the table (if anything) at any given time.

If you are running a large company or network as a general manager, or EVP, or president, the EDO results from each individual office will be a great eye opener to objectively judge the business acumen and the effectiveness of each one of your managers. The difference between the best and the not-so-great can be overwhelming. (See EDO graphic)

At the top of the form, you need to just look at your physical plant:

- How many desks do you have?
- How many agents do you have?
- Based on the above, what is your occupancy percentage?
- For example, if you have 72 desks and 92 associates, the occupancy factor is 127.8%.
- Then, you look at your financial statements for the year or any number of months:
- What are total operating expenses (payroll, building/ equipment, advertising, eventual allocation, etc.)?
- How many desks do you have?
- Based on the above, what is your cost per desk?
- For example, if your annual operating expenses amount to $1,800,000 and you have 72 desks, the desk cost is $25k/ year. In other words, theoretically, every agent would need to produce $25,000 in company dollars (House part of the split) to pay for his/her desk

For the fun of it, you may also want to know the company dollar amount each agent needs to produce irrespective as to the total number of desks or, for that matter, whether the office has desks

EFFECTIVE DESK OCCUPANCY

Office: _____ **Manager:** _____ **Period:** 2020

Desk #: 20 **Agents:** 24 **Occupancy:** 120%

Operating Expenses: $500,000 **Annual Desk Cost:** $25K

Jo $175K	**Mary** $150K	**Linda** $125K	**Bruce** $100K
Alan $75K	**Karen** $50K	**Susan** $40K	**Oscar** $30K
Bruno $25K	**Max** $20K / **Janet** $8K	**John** $17K / **Maurice** $9K	**Bill** $15K / **Anne** $10K
Rick $12K / Doug $11K / Lynn $4K	Greg $10K / Bob $7K / Marcia $5K / Frank $3.5K	Lynda $8K / Rita $2K	0
0	0	0	0

 # Desks Fully Covered: 14 **EDO:** 70%

or not.

If we used the same numbers listed above ($1.8M in expenses and 92 associates, the cost per agent would be $19,565.

Fill the boxes

The next step is to design a diagram of your office illustrated by a box for each physical desk. To keep things simple (and for lack of space), the graphic used is only showing 20 boxes.

Considering that each box is worth $25k in company dollars, the questions are:

- Who (agent's name) is paying the "rent", so to speak?
- How many of your associates cover the desk cost?
- If a box is not fully paid for by an agent, add another agent's contribution to fill the gap until you reach the $25k minimum. In some cases, it may take three or four agents to cover the cost of a desk.

At the end of the exercise, you will have a clear visual of your overall office performance.

Although your desk occupancy percentage at, say, 120%, may suggest that you are doing a terrific job at recruiting, you may find that your EDO percentage is "only" 70%. 30% of the associates do not produce enough commission dollars for the office to cover desk cost. In other words, you need more agents, or better ones, or a combination of the two.

The fact that you may be in the profit zone is great but it is only because you have a few superstars who bring a heck of a lot more dollars to the office cash register than their individual share is calling for. It should not hide the fact that you have a lot of "producers" who are lagging behind in the red zone. If you rely too much on top agents to pay the bills, you rely on the unreliable.

Remember, an office is never full. The recruiting never ends.

The idea is not just to hire for the sake of hiring, the idea is to make money with the people that you have.

If you do, try to do better.

If you don't, you better do better.

No matter what, as a general rule, you always need more agents than you have desks for. That's the beginning. If you are not there yet, you are not even on the starting line to fight for a great EDO.

Chapter 7

Office Checkup

If you are running a large organization with multiple offices, you are constantly challenging yourself to follow the performance of each one. What is the added value of each profit center to the overall well-being of the company? Several factors need to be periodically (at a minimum once a year) looked at and evaluated:

- The location of the office
- Its size, layout, functionality and equipment
- The market environment – the competition
- The manager – Right one?

Every one of the above considerations is permanently on your radar as changes may need to be made to remain competitive in the marketplace.

We'll deal with the "managers' effectiveness" in a separate chapter. In this one, we will use the flashlight and the magnifying glass to look at the other factors which can affect the success of an office.

The Office Checkup could look as follows (keep it short and simple):

Office 1 (Town name)
Status and pulse:
- Small fish in a big pond
- Not the best location. Hard to find. Parking issue
- Friendly group of agents, most of them committed to the company
- Low level of production due to above factors

Recommendations:
- Need new, spacious and well-located office ASAP to grab a decent share of the market, particularly at the high-end.

Office 2 (Town name)

Status and pulse:
- #1 office in the local market
- Fine location. Newly renovated and expanded office
- Very busy turnover market with abundant inventory of affordable properties. Should be a good money maker in foreseeable future
- Good mix of agents – Friendly atmosphere
- Outstanding administrative staff

Recommendations:
- OK for now – Don't make waves

Office 3 (Town name)

Status and pulse:
- #3 office in the local market
- Adequate location, although inferior to that of company Q and company M
- Attractive office fits the image of the upper end communities it caters to
- Mostly young and inexperienced associates with little loyalty to the company
- Lack of routine prospecting activities

Recommendations:
- Need stronger agents and hopefully one or two franchise players
- Do we have the right manager?

Office 4 (Town name)

Status and pulse:
- Market leader – a flagship for the company

- Best, newly renovated office, capable of housing over 90 agents
- Mostly old timers, highly qualified and successful
- Good busy working environment
- Great staff at the front desk

Recommendations:

- None at this point

Office 5 (Town name)

Status and pulse:

- Good downtown location with excellent walk-in traffic
- Mostly new people
- Production potential commensurate with small square footage and low experience level of associates

Recommendations:

- Try to find a larger pad in same downtown location
- Think about closing the office or using it as a satellite location for Office 4

Office 6 (Town name)

Status and pulse:

- Outstanding location and office facilities
- Newer office but populated with young, smart and action-oriented agents
- Will soon become the regional powerhouse in terms of units, if not volume (low average sales price)

Recommendations:

- Help agents with their marketing
- Provide more training and workshops

Office 7 (Town name)

Status and pulse:

- #2 office in the local market
- Excellent corner location with great visibility and parking

galore
- Strong loyal and homogeneous group of agents – highly spirited warriors
- Good turnover market

Recommendations:
- None

Office 8 (Town name)

Status and pulse:
- #1 office in local high-end market
- Prime location but about to be lost (within six months) due to purchase of property by developer
- The new office, within 300 ft, is a year away
- Many top producers are a bit antsy at the prospect of changing location and considering the dead time between closure of the office and the opening of new one

Recommendations:
- Stay close to the top producers – offer help with marketing
- Use staff to keep ears and eyes open regarding the morale of the troops
- Find good space (in existing office?) to relocate agents in between offices

Office 9 (Town name)

Status and pulse:
- Fluctuates between #2 and #3 position in market.
- Too small a space considering our recruiting needs and size and velocity of the local market
- Good nucleus of stars in the making – lots of bright prospecting ideas but not enough leg work

Recommendations:
- Need bigger space ASAP

Office 10 (Town name)

Status and pulse:

- Nice modern facilities, greatly enhanced by the recent addition
- Friendly office comprised mostly of hard-working associates
- Best farming office taking advantage of market makeup and high turnover

Recommendations:

- None at this point

Chapter 8

Office Sales Managers' Checkup

Of all the job positions one can hold in a real estate organization, the most pivotal, without a doubt, is that of office/branch manager.

It is not easy to succeed in such position, as you need to please two masters. On one side the associates who can devour your time, brains, energy, and can leave you cold any day for good or no-good reasons. On the other, upper-management who does not care as much about what you do and how you do it so long that money keeps on pouring into the cash register.

When you do succeed however, there is no better job on earth and none that is more critical to the stability and the growth of a company.

I often say that agents, however great they may be, are only as good as the company they are with. Indeed, the company has a full toolbox and lots of associates, such that it does not depend on any one agent.

In the case of a manager, it's a different ballgame. A great manager can actually be "better" than his/her company. Such manager can be so influential than he/she can inspire upper-management and possibly transform the company.

With only rare exceptions, an office or a company cannot "make" the manager, but it can be said that a powerful manager can make the office/company.

Nice to be loved

I remember fondly my years as an office manager. My happiest real estate years probably, come to think of it. "My" associates were my friends and I believe they too considered me a friend. The team was so solid, so "together," so driven, so powerful that our main challenge was to keep on beating our own records.

As a result, upper-management was sweet and caring, so much so that I felt guilty being paid for my work (although I never said no to another bonus or accolade). Nice to be loved.

Having said that, I sometimes wonder why someone would ever want to become a manager in this cut-throat business, and what it takes to succeed. Managers are all unique. There is no such thing as a standard office manager.

Depending on the size and performance of the company or network, managers emerge from different breeding grounds. Three mostly:

- *Homegrown manager:* Nice way to reward a company associate who shines with the right production, skills, attitude, and ambition. It reinforces the company pride/ spirit and encourages other agents to emulate the rookie manager. Also on the plus side is the fact that the agent knows and is already sold on the company programs, services, policies and procedures. This will help transitioning from soldier to commander in chief.
- One concern though: if the agent was a top producer, as it is usually the case, he/she is likely to take a significant "pay" cut and get cold feet after a while. Beware. I know that, in my case, the income drop was like a blood bath. I took the offer though. It's only money.
- *Superstar agent coming from the competition:* Very tempting as he/she is admired and respected by the agents right from the start. They like the fact that the company attracts winners and they are anxious to learn from the new manager, at least during the honeymoon period.
- Risky move for the firm however, and not just because of the income wake up call. Who says transfer from another brokerage says change of culture, if not culture shock. The newbie might not fit. He/she may quit or be "excused"

after just a few weeks or months, which can be very damaging to the agents' morale. They (and the company) will be more cautious or even more skeptical next time.

- *Existing manager from another company:* Looks like a nice coup at first. After all, if we seduce and soon "steal" a manager from the competition, we stand to attract many of his/her former associates who may feel abandoned by the boss and shave significant market share from the losing competitor. What's not to like?

This scenario, however appealing, is not much safer than playing Russian roulette though. Why? For a host of reasons. For one, you may wonder why this manager accepted to work for your brand. Might be curiosity or envy, or might just be more money, which might be a red flag since a bigger carrot is always available somewhere. Some probing is necessary to find his/her motivation for changing flag.

I can assure you that if you can "buy" a competitor, someone else can and probably will indeed buy him/her again. Some people are always "for sale" and live with their suitcase ready, keeping an eye open for the next opportunity.

Checkup

Managers, like everyone else, change over time. They may get better or it can go the other way.

They may stay and proudly retire with their company hat on, or lose their mojo, or move far away, or quit the profession for good, or return to sales, or again decide to join the competition to see if the grass is greener on the other side. You never know.

As a general manager, an EVP, president, or as an owner, you have to keep your ears to the ground and listen to the vibrations. You just have to be prepared at the risk of having a manager suddenly switch to low gear or leave overnight with possible devastating consequences.

It's only good business to regularly take the pulse of every office and review the managers' strong and weak points. With proper support and coaching, weaker managers can dramatically improve. Good managers can improve even more since they are great to begin with and may only need help in a few minor areas.

That's the job of upper-management to be sensitive to the needs and respond accordingly.

That's the purpose of the following "managers' checkup" which should preferably be done twice a year, or no less than once a year. Such checkup can be added to the "office checkup" which has been reviewed in a separate chapter.

Karen – Office 1
- *Strengths*: Great company person/asset. Loyal, sincere, dependable and committed to the growth and success of the company in her marketplace. She is a giver in a mother-type way, always attentive to caring for her agents. Very knowledgeable about the business. Enjoys recruiting and is good at it.
- *Weaknesses*: Being that she is a bit of a perfectionist and a control freak, she can be easily destabilized when things go wrong in the office. Her reactions to a crisis can be too authoritarian rather than taking the long view, try to understand the problem and deal with it one agent at a time and with diplomacy.
- *Recommendations*: Could use some coaching (Albert) and a mix of direction and support (me).

Lisa – Office 2
- *Strengths*: Everybody's best friend. An agent at heart, very understanding of the needs and wants of her people. Inspires trust. Very good with numbers, business matters and technology. Proud representative of the family. Confident.

- *Weaknesses*: Too soft at this point to exert the direction that some of her agents need to go to the next level. Tendency to devote too much time with a handful of good agents (friends) and not enough with those who can use her management skills and time to feel part of the team and more connected to the company.
- *Recommendations*: management training where she can learn as much from her peers than from the "trainer". She is getting a lot out of the regional meetings/round table discussions.

Harry – Office 3

- *Strengths*: All American, very likable and approachable guy. Presents well. Good business mind. Ambitious and anxious to do well, as much for the sake of money as for the need to be recognized for what he does.
- *Weaknesses*: Still a novice trying to become popular by saying yes rather than being effective by saying no. A bit weak in terms of real estate knowledge and management skills. Still learning how to "sell" activities that result in income (SOI/Open houses...).
- *Recommendations*: He is getting all he needs with me helping him in real time with strategy, analysis, planning, etc.

Mary – Office 4

- *Strengths*: Great very rounded and hands-on manager. What you see is what you get: an inspirational and dynamic leader who walks the talk and motivates her agents to work hard and smart. Excellent at driving company or office programs and at recruiting.
- *Weaknesses*: tendency to go after quantity rather than quality when it comes to listings/sales as well as recruits. This results in spreading her transactions over too many

markets which do not create recurring business and not getting her fair share of the high-end market she so badly needs.

- *Recommendations*: No problem, she is learning with huge appetite and is thrilled at the prospect of getting better.

Max – Office 5

- *Strengths*: Intelligent and articulate manager, liked and well respected by agents. Good thinker and problem solver. Good at one-on-one meetings where he can best show support and understanding. Effective also at sales meetings. Like a turtle, he is slow at getting anywhere but he always gets there.
- *Weaknesses*: Needs to focus on his primary market where the office is near non-existent. It means getting the right people to consistently do the bulk of their activities in the right market and with the right tools. It will take time and persistence but he should win that challenge.
- *Recommendations*: Stay on his back to keep him focused and work with him to help him recruit true local players who can blanket the town with mailings.

Lynda – Office 6

- *Strengths*: Good sense of business. Analytical. Very personable. Not afraid and in fact eager to use other peoples' brains to do better. Proud of the company and good at selling our vision to the agents.
- *Weaknesses*: Lacks dynamism, drive and resolve. Not using her business mind near as much as she should to mobilize her agents and get them to do more to achieve success. Slow at recruiting. Does not put in a full day.
- *Recommendations*: work with training staff on goal setting and planning activities in order to reach goals. I will need to assist her as a "back seat manager" to wake up the

potential of the office.

Joe – Office 7

- *Strengths*: Knowledgeable, no nonsense, sophisticated. Good image and good brain.
- *Weaknesses*: Too skeptical about the value of hiring brand new people, although she badly needs new blood, new energy in an office dominated by associates about to retire.
- *Recommendations*: Work with her on a six-month recruiting plan with specific monthly objectives. If necessary, hire recruiting assistant or use a specialized outside service.

David – Office 8

- *Strengths*: He is our flag bearer in the county. Loyal, reliable, effective. Profit oriented. Self-motivated. Inspires trust, confidence.
- *Weaknesses*: Needs to focus and promote geographic farming.
- *Recommendations*: None at this point.

Chapter 9

Areas of Expertise

It does not take a genius to notice that, although we may agree that all office sales managers are born equal, they don't stay that way very long. They evolve in many different ways and at a much different speed. Some managers grow up to be good at what they are supposed to do for a living, some eventually become very good, and some have some work to do to justify the title and keep the job.

To be fair, it is not easy to manage, whatever it is that managers have to manage. So let's pause for a minute and brainstorm about exactly that: what it is that office sales managers actually have to manage.

Having been around a while, living with managers or watching them from various points of observation, I reached the conclusion that, to be most effective in their functions, managers need to be as good as they can be in four different areas of expertise:

- They need to be good with people
- They need to be good with numbers
- They need to be good with time and priorities
- They need to be good with "things" or "stuff."

Now, for the million-dollar question: are all managers comfortable and, more importantly, proficient in all four of such diverse disciplines and skills? No. Would be nice alright but, alas, perfection is not a common trait of the human kind, managers or not.

And that's OK. It takes all kinds. Some managers may get an A+ in one category and only passing grade in the others. Might be good enough, as long as their weaknesses do not affect too much the performance of the office and they manage to keep the trust of both upper-management and the agents.

Of course, it depends which area of expertise they excel at, or, to put it the other way, in which areas they are lagging behind and how far behind?

With this in mind, let's review the relative importance of each one of the four categories, starting with the last one on the list.

Things or stuff

By "things" or "stuff," I mean everything apart from people, numbers, and time. In other words, office sales managers need to be good at "managing" marketing, technology, training, relocation, company programs, ancillary services, policies, procedures, etc. A lot. A basket full of different specialties.

All the above mentioned "things" are incredibly important to be sure, but they are primarily handled by others, department heads or senior executives who are directly responsible for their creation or revision and accountable for their success.

All the so-called office managers need to do, at their level, is to clearly understand the various subjects and carry the torch to the next stage. They have to sell the company's choices/decisions to the troops and insure optimum implementation.

After all, the manager is the representative of the various department heads and VP's in the office. As such, he/she must be knowledgeable, convinced, and convincing. If not, chances are the company programs are likely to be ignored and fail miserably. Time to look for another manager?

Time – Priorities

Nothing too terribly scientific about this one. There is only so much time in the day and, as we say, time is money. It needs to be spent intelligently. It takes a while for new managers to understand what that means.

New and bad managers, eager to please, deal first with what comes next, whether an agent rushing into the manager's office or a new phone call, no matter how significant or insignificant it might be. You know the type. That's the best way for managers to get in a bottleneck of their own making and create what HR may refer to as crisis management. Not good.

Obviously, priorities must be defined in terms of their degree of importance to the wellbeing of the business. Urgencies, in a busy real estate office, are known to occasionally interfere with a planned agenda but, for the most part, the items marked in red on the day calendar need to be dealt with before those in yellow and whatever else demands attention and resolution.

Nice to have an open-door policy but it's not an invitation to disturb at will. There are some exceptions that a smart manager should share with all agents early on as to avoid upsetting impatient or hot tempered top producers.

Numbers

That's what it's all about. The end result. What we all work for, as a company, as an office, as a manager, as an agent. Money-money. Don't we all like that word?

In a way, the bottom-line numbers, like all production or financial numbers on a business plan or a P&L, are the result of what the manager does in the other three categories of expertise. If the multidimensional job is done well (and assuming that the market cooperates), the numbers will look good. If not, well, several options are always on the table.

Either way, the office manager is accountable for the results… Even when he/she is not completely in charge of the operations. That's the job. It is rightfully expected that the manager understands numbers, know what activities they derive from and what needs to be done in order to deliver on the plan. (This key subject is well covered in other chapters of the book)

People

If there is one area of expertise which is not optional in our business, it spells P.E.O.P.L.E. Nothing is more critically important for the obvious reason that it takes people/agents to sell real estate. No agents = no listings = no sales = no revenues = no office.

If the manager does not have the necessary people skills and a true honest affection as well as respect for the agents, the office will indeed quickly become a lonely place with only two survivors (for a short while): the "manager" and a paid receptionist. Next, the "closed" sign will soon appear on the front door.

The wellbeing of a real estate office depends, first and foremost, on the relationship between the manager and the sales associates. If and when the agents get a lot of qualified support and care from the manager (and the administrative people), life is good and business can click.

This bond, based on trust and mutual appreciation, builds loyalty and alleviate or cure most problems. Peace and happiness on earth. When the agents are content, they feel engaged, energized, and they fight for the manager and the company as much as they fight for themselves. Well, close to it.

That's the perfect recipe for success. People always come first. Somehow, business follows and numbers have a chance to come out looking fine.

Chapter 10

Culture

As an active protagonist in the field of real estate management for a good number of years, I have always been fascinated by the lack of emphasis most companies' owners or top leaders place on culture.

To me, the company culture is the cement that brings and keeps people together, regardless of their position and pay grade. It is the spirit that causes managers, staff and agents to move in the same direction, animated by the feeling of belonging to the right firm and the same desire to win for the team.

OK, perhaps I am making too much of very little. What do you think, as a manager?

What is your definition of culture? Who is it for? What purpose does it serve?

Let's talk about your real estate company, shall we?

What is its vision, if it has any?

What is its mission, if it has any?

What are its core values and principles, if it has any?

What is its culture, if it has any?

OK, now, as a Realtor and sales manager, what about your own vision, values, and principles?

Do they align with that of your brokerage firm? Does it matter to you that you believe in your company's culture or would you rather that your company had none? Why are you associated with your company rather than with another?

Making money is what any business (whether a company, an office, a manager or an agent) is about. The goal is the same because, at the end of the day, if you don't make more than you spend, you have to close the shop.

But money, as we all know, does not flow just because it's

a lofty goal. It flows, if and when it does, because we have a winning business model and philosophy and we are good enough to attract and inspire agents, sellers, and buyers who want a piece of the success story.

Hi-tech examples

When it comes to culture, it is interesting to observe and study what the most successful hi-tech companies are doing to compete for the best brains in the field.

Some have a great deal of success in attracting talent by offering, for free, all kinds of terrific foods to the employees, 24/7. Some offer baby-sitting services, free cleaning/laundry, free lodging for a number of months.

Some, even more aggressive, offer recruiting bonuses or a chunk of the stock, which can be very juicy if the company is on the road to a successful IPO. Some are more spiritual, contributing large sums to charitable causes.

Culture has a price

It takes all kinds. Same thing for real estate companies. For some real estate companies that is, those which have a personality, a style, a true culture.

Those companies exist but force is to recognize that the number is shrinking. For one thing, culture has a price. Many are the companies that can't or don't care to pay to preserve it.

Also, culture can only exist and shine if ownership and management, up and down the ladder, stand firm behind it and promote it each and every day. If managers of the same firm do business differently, there is no company culture.

In my judgment, company culture, in the real estate business, is more a word than a fact. It is an inspirational light that is progressively going dark.

Lots of reasons for that, as mentioned above. No matter what it is, it tends to make companies look alike and act alike for the agents.

The company way

Are companies becoming interchangeable? They preach one thing but may do another. Some of their leaders pursue different agendas and prefer to take the easy road rather than promote core values.

Many of the most critical responsibilities and competitive advantages of a real estate company are often delegated or outsourced to intermediaries which do not necessarily share the same principles or objectives.

Take training and coaching as an example. Teaching is THE company's opportunity to differentiate itself from competitors, putting its culture stamp on all aspects of the business.

What we often see, however, is that most companies go through the generic exercise of teaching the right things but not necessarily teaching the right way, the company way.

This has actually become a paradigm in our industry. I am talking about the huge success of professional business coaches, speaking gurus touring the country from one end of the calendar to the other, and evangelizing thousands of managers and/or agents from different states, markets and companies on how to work in the real estate business.

Not only are participants paying good money to hear the words of wisdom but most real estate top leaders are promoting these events, as if they were their own, and encourage the agents to sign up while demanding that sales managers do the same.

A culture which is mass-promoted and implemented by outsiders is not a company culture.

Real estate firms are not born equal

Don't get me wrong, I too see lots of value in agents and managers attending mega-superstars coaching/training venues.

The few very successful speakers on the tour are amazing people and several are friends of mine.

They get results: those agents who listen are so energized that they do what they are being told. They are disciplined enough to plan their days, make the cold calls, knock on doors, practice their scripts, generate leads, secure appointments, get listings, and make sales. They are contributing to any and all companies' success.

Pretty good right? After all, agents are only as good as what they do and they sure do what outside coaches tell them to do.

The problem is that the same message, ideas, scripts, words, tactics... are dispensed to thousands at a time, irrespective of geographic market, affiliation, identity, image, values... culture.

Teaching agents to chase units and close deals is great. It pays the agents and the brokers' bills, but it also levels the field and dilutes the value of working for one company vs. another. Not a good way to build loyalty.

Think about this: is the way you work based on your company's culture, or is your company's culture based on the way you work?

Real estate firms are not born equal. They do not grow the same way. Each follows its unique path, unless they choose to depend more on others for direction.

Company culture and mass culture often clash and when they do, mass produced culture (if there is such a thing) usually wins.

To protect your own, you have to promote it. It never ends, unless your own story ends.

Chapter 11

Management vs. Leadership

Management and leadership, two magic words in the business world in general and in the field of real estate in particular. Often, one is used to describe the other, as if the two were interchangeable. That, they are not.

Bear with me for a little while, I'll try to offer a few thoughts and tips on how to best distinguish between the two. Then, hopefully, you will have an easier time finding out which of the two words more appropriately corresponds to you today and which one of the two you would rather identify with.

One way to start is to recognize that "manager" is a title or a function, while "leader" is a recognition, a quality of sorts. Apple and orange. You can mix them up to make a good smoothie but you should not confuse the two. The word "leadership" is overused and, more often than not, misused.

Another defining point of difference is what each one of the two words applies to.

In my opinion, formed over a lifetime of management and leadership, management applies mostly to "things." You can manage an office, you can manage numbers, you can manage activities, you can manage your time, etc. But what about people? Can you manage agents?

In my experience, you can only manage one person at a time. You can manage a real estate office, a region, a company but it would be illusory to believe that you could manage all or any large group of agents within anyone of these corporate entities.

If and when you do, there is another word to use: "leadership."

In my book, the most interesting distinction between management and leadership in the real estate industry is this one:

Upper management makes you a manager, but the agents make you a leader.

Characteristics and qualities

A good manager follows the company's direction, relays the message to the troops with persuasion albeit with a personal touch, and tries to deliver on the company's expectations. That's a job, clearly defined and paid accordingly. It is not an easy job. Managers represent the essential communication link between the top and the base.

Office sales managers have two bosses: upper-management or ownership full of expectations on one side and, on the other, independent agents/field soldiers who often think they are generals.

Knowledge, focus, control, reliability and accountability are characteristics often associated with the position, regardless what the management level is. There is always someone or something above anyone of us.

Good managers are rare and, as such, wanted. All companies need winners. Real estate is an incredibly competitive and predatory business, so the hunt to find winners is as hot as the fight to keep them.

Very good managers can also be good/strong leaders. Some, in fact, may be better leaders than the people running the company if and when the big chiefs are so preoccupied by the bottom-line numbers that they neglect to pay attention to the managers and agents who produce them.

Interestingly enough, leaders are not necessarily good managers. They tend to be more conceptually minded than detail oriented. In that case, they have to find good managers to handle the operations.

When they are great at both, they are worth gold in the business. They are the thinkers and the doers in the same package.

What's a leader?

The definition is something like "a leader is someone people follow." Correction: "a leader is someone people want to follow."

Pretty simple, right? Well, may be a bit too simple. If it were that simple, leaders would grow like rabbits and populate every sector of every business and industry. All would-be leaders would need to do to earn the coveted "title" and attract a crowd of followers, is to buddy up with the troops and let them do whatever they want, including nothing.

Leadership is not about making friends for the sake of it or acquiescing to unreasonable and unjustified requests to buy respect and loyalty. A true leader can be (and usually is) tough-minded and demanding. And it's fine, as long that he/she is also just, fair, honest, sincere, and consistent.

Agents like and need to be challenged. They do not respect managers who are not holding them accountable and/or who are too weak to motivate them to be better. They need a manager's attention but they also crave for a leader.

There is quite a long list of needed magic ingredients to describe leadership. Those that jump off the page are:

- Exciting, clear, believable and contagious vision. Tactics can change, strategy can be tweaked, but vision transcends both.
- Inspiration. It is the engine that creates faith. It drives people/believers to new heights. Motivation comes and goes; inspiration lasts.
- Trust. As long as the agents genuinely trust the leader and are sold on his/her vision, they will accept the vision as their own. They will fight for the leader with the highest degree of conviction.
- Charisma. Leaders always have interesting, if not intriguing style and personality, thus reinforcing their influence over others.

- Communication. Key to rallying the troops. Leaders are generally great communicators and know how to captivate and mobilize an audience.
- Brains. It sure helps to be smart and, if possible, a well-rounded scholar of sort to make believers and continually drive success
- Passion. You feel it. It is the fuel that moves people to extraordinary achievements.

And, to a lesser degree:

- Ambition. The focused desire or need to strive for more and better achievements
- Humility. Not a prerequisite to qualify but much appreciated. The cherry on the cake
- Two more tips before we close the subject.

Competing managers

If you are a "selling" office manager and expect to be a true leader, you may want to sit down with yourself and think long and hard about what's wrong with this picture. How can you inspire the trust of your agents if you "compete" with them for listings and/or sales?

Your abilities in so doing are not questioned. You don't have to show how good you are in a job which is no longer yours. If you want to make incremental money for yourself and the office, show how good you are at making your associates even better. That's how, ultimately, you will and should be judged as a manager.

One thing though that you can do to show how good you are in a sales capacity and rightfully inspire your agents: go with them on listing presentations and do your show. Amaze them. That's the best coaching any manager can do.

It's pretty gutsy though. You want to shine and win, not look like you don't know what you are doing, and possibly screw up a listing opportunity for the agent you mean to help.

This challenge, that you would do "for free," has both a management value and a true leadership value. It keeps you honest and eager to keep up to speed on the agents' job since you have skin in the game.

From an agent's point of view, this could very well be the best link in between management and leadership.

Chapter 12

Business Plans – Agents

One of my favorite topics. A most important one for managers to be sure. After all, their own individual office business plan is - or should be - the combined sum of the associates' expectations (minus the delta between dreams and likely reality...).

Sales agents need to have a business mind. They are in business. They work for themselves. They are independent contractors.

Like any and all entrepreneurs, they have to think 24/7 about what they should do, what they can do, and what they commit to doing.

They are only as good as what they do.

Every morning, they have to open their virtual shop and stand ready and prepared to do business: meet clients, prospect for more, advertise, and plan for the next day. If they sleep in a bit too much or call it a day, the dollars are not going to pile up in the cash register.

Some agents are self-motivated, responsible, organized, mobilized, and goal oriented. Some are not. What happens, happens. If it does not, well, there is always another day.

To be meaningful and realistic, an annual goal must be "dissected" into pieces: months, weeks or days. The to-do list of tasks, for every day, translates into weekly and monthly objectives. When you add them up, you've got a business plan.

The job of a manager is of course critical in the agents' planning process. They are managers for a reason. They need to instill in their associates the value and even the imperatives of setting clear achievement objectives and calendar them through the year. There is a lot of explaining to do to get them to understand the process and to hold them accountable for the results.

Activities driven

There are basically two ways for real estate agents to approach goal setting

- Set the desired year-end result, like the total commission income (the carrot) or the total dollar sales volume of sales
- Commit to specific business activities each and every month and see what they yield at the end of the year in the way of revenue and volume of sales.

From experience, I tend to disregard the first option. It often equates to dreaming. A plan like this is not a plan. Most agents, particularly newer agents and weak agents don't have any idea about what it would take to achieve their "goals."

They may shoot for an arbitrary goal of $300k even though they only made $50k the year before. Or, by excess of modesty or innocence, they may set the goal at $55k based on their $50k prior accomplishments. Both goals are irrelevant since they are based on empty wishes rather than what these agents are committed to doing to make their objectives come true.

As for the second option, based on regular activities, it looks more like a winner. I am 100% sold on it. As I wrote earlier, agents are only as good as what they do. If they do a lot and do it well, they get good results; if they don't, they are crossing the desert at night time without a compass.

In this case, it is perfectly doable to go from a mediocre income one year to a fabulous income the following year since the business plan is built on regular committed activities. Up to the agent and the manager to follow the plan and deliver on the expectations.

What activities?

Whatever creates business opportunities. Name your sport.

The best one I know is weekend open houses. It does not cost a penny and can produce thousands of dollars. A no-brainer activity for new and experienced agents alike. Best and easiest way to meet prospective buyers and sellers (See separate chapter on the subject).

There are dozens of other activities for your agents to commit to. I will only list a few:

- Geographic farming (newsletters, mailings, emails, tweets, calls, visits, parties, etc.): monthly goals
- Social SOIs (spheres of influence): same
- Just listed/just sold cards: used after each new transaction. Hit the entire neighborhood and your SOI
- Cold calls: daily task. Go down a pre-established list, use a good script and think fast on your feet. The idea is to make appointments ASAP
- Advertising: great visibility in your primary market. Stay in the public eye. Build your image/brand. Promote yourself or your listings or both. Attracts both buyers and sellers.

Business plan models

I have seen many (too many) suggested models and forms. Confusing as heck. Some business plans' models have three, four, five, or more, pages. They are so detailed and complicated that they can take hours to study and a few more to fill out. Not to mention the time it will take to review.

Some list a bunch of questions and warnings on the various costs associated with the job, like car expenses, Board and MLS dues, E&O, administrative/technology fees, marketing/prospecting, etc.

I don't like negative stuff in a business plan. Sure it's

important for agents to take into consideration the cost of doing business and they do, but the focus should be what they plan on doing to make money rather than spend money to do what they plan on doing.

Some models are so lengthy and intimidating that it would be easier and more fun to fill out an application for a mortgage loan.

My choice of format is simple: one page. Period. And I recommend that you, as a manager, choose such model as well.

Let's be honest: do you really have the time to critic and analyze an agent's ten-page business plan? Do you really want to take the time, each and every month or so, to review all the pages and monitor all the listed activities and expenses?

No, you don't. Don't kid yourself. You probably have many associates, meaning many plans to review. You are not a personal tutor, you've got an office to run.

A good business plan is a visual. One that the agent can look at daily to know what to do and how to track the results.

As a manager, you can use the same visual to follow the agents' activities. You can do it easily at a glance since everything is on a single page.

Plan format

(See sample table and an example of a completed plan)

The typical plan should be composed of 14 columns: the first one for the totals achieved the year before, the last one for the expected and actual totals for this year and, in between, one for each of the twelve months of the year.

For the good reasons stated before, the activities are listed first. They have to. They run the show. They drive the business. Everything else is just a result of the activities.

The form follows the normal business cycle: prospecting to transactions to financial numbers.

As such, the first four lines identify prospecting activities.

MY 2020 BUSINESS PLAN

ABC Realty

Name: _____ Office: _____

2019 TOTALS	Activities = Income	JAN	FEB	MAR	APR	MAY	JUN	JUL	AUG	SEP	OCT	NOV	DEC	TOTALS
36	# O.H. / Prim. Mkt	3/1	3/1	4/1	4/2	4/2	5/2	4/2	3/2	4/2	5/2	5/3	3/2	47/22
	Actual	3/2	3/1	4/2	5/3	5/3								
0	# SOI Mailings / Prim.Mkt	500/300	500/300	500/300	500/300	500/300	500/300	500/300	500/300	500/400	500/400	500/400	500/400	6K/4K
	Actual	300/0	500/200	500/200	500/200	500/300								
700	# Just Listed / Just Sold	0	100	100	100	150	150			200	200	200	200	1,400
	Actual	0	0	100	100	100								
8	# Promo / Ads	0	0	2	2	2	2	1		3	3	3	2	20
	Actual	0	1	1	1	0								
10	# Listings	1	1	2	2	3	3	3	2	3	3	3	2	28
	Actual	0	1	1	2	2								
18	# Open Sales	1	2	2	2	3	3	2	2	2	3	3	2	27
	Actual	0	0	1	2	2								
17	# Closed Sales	0	2	2	2	3	3	2	2	2	3	2	2	26
	Actual	1	1	2	1	2								
720K	Average Sale Price	800K	800K	800K	800K	800K	800K	800K	800K	800K	800K	800K	800K	800K
	Actual	700K	800K	900K	850K	800K								
11,550K	$ Volume of Sales	0	1600K	1600K	1600K	2400K	2400K	1600K	1600K	1600K	2400K	2400K	1600K	20,800K
	Actual	700K	800K	1800K	850K	1600K								
2.70%	Commission Rate %	2.75%	2.75%	2.75%	2.75%	2.75%	2.75%	2.75%	2.75%	2.75%	2.75%	2.75%	2.75%	2.75%
311,850	Gross Commission $	19,250	22,000	49,500	23,375	44,000	66,000	44,000	44,000	44,000	66,000	66,000	44,000	532,125
72%	My Average Split %	75%	75%	75%	75%	75%	78%	78%	78%	80%	80%	80%	85%	78%
224,532	My Net Income	14,438	16,500	37,125	17,531	33,000	51,480	34,320	34,320	35,200	52,800	52,800	37,400	416,914

Date Prepared: *June 1 - (5 months of actual results)*   Associate's Signature: _____   Manager's Signature: _____

Comments:

You should add, delete, or modify the list according to your priorities.

The first line is about open houses, my pet activity. The agent can list the number he/she commits to doing during the month and how many of those belong to the local/primary market. Once the month is over, the agent can write, underneath, the number of open houses actually held.

Same principle for the next three activities. First the agent lists the number of mailings/cards/ads/calls and later jots down what, in fact, he/she has completed. Easy to do, easy to read, easy to track.

Next, the expected and somewhat logical results of the above activities: the contracts.

The first item is "listings." That's where it starts. You can't sell if there is nothing to sell. Of course, only those listed by the agent are mentioned on the form.

Then come the sales expected through the twelve months. Sales deriving from the agent's listings and sales of competitors' listings. "Open sales" come first, followed by "closed sales."

Allow roughly 10% of waste. Not all listings are going to sell and not all sales are going to make it to closing. This is why there is a "closed sales" box.

On the completed form I attached, you will note that there is, for the most part, a thirty-day time correlation between new listings and open sales and another such time deferral between open sales and closed sales. The assumption here is that the market is pretty good: listings sell within a month and sales close within thirty days. Up to you to adjust for your market, depending on the business conditions.

The six items to follow are about the money. The good part.

On the plan, each agent has to scientifically guess an average price, based on where he/she does the shopping and then multiply the number of closed deals that month to come up with the volume of sales.

Using an expected commission rate to arrive at a total Gross commission and then a split, the agent can discover what he/she stands to make for the month and, a few columns further, for the whole year.

Surprises

When you build a business plan from top to bottom, from activities to earned dollars, agents may find two surprises (hopefully good ones):

- They may find that the expected results (income, units and volume) are far different from the corresponding numbers they put on the books the year before. For example, an agent may be a bit perplexed "discovering" that he/she projects to earn $250,000 when, last year, he/she made only $45,000. That's the beauty of the activities' driven plan: as we said earlier, the resulting income is based on what one does and not of what one made in the past. The past income is absolutely not relevant if based on an arbitrary goal rather than specific tasks/activities.

  An income goal does not mean a thing if the agent does not know how to achieve it.
- For related reasons, most agents who follow the order of the one-page business plan will be surprised to see that they can make more than they anticipated. If nothing else, it will motivate them to scrupulously adhere to their own commitments.

If, however, the plan totals do not quite match their ambitious expectations, all they have to do with your help is walk back through the form and tweak one or more indicators to create additional revenue.

For example, they may increase their open house or mailings numbers to produce more transactions, or choose to farm in an area where prices average $1.5M instead of $800K to pocket the incremental revenue.

Business plans are tailored to the individuals' needs and means as well as their expectations. Your job, as a manager, is first to make sure all agents fully understand the value of planning and the process to follow. You will accompany and support them along the way, month after month, to keep them on track.

I suggest you explain the "rules" at your weekly sales meeting, distribute blank copies of the business plan and go over each item/line.

The agents have to recognize that, for their plan to be realistic and therefore doable, the itinerary (the activities) they will follow is more meaningful than the destination at this point. The end result is entirely predicated on what they do to make it to the finish line.

Commitments mean something and accountability is a must.

Chapter 13

Business Plans – Managers

A long time ago, when I got the job of running an office as a sales manager and had to put some reasonably intelligent numbers on a business plan, I created a form that I used all my professional life as a real estate leader. I called the form "Dashboard."

I can guarantee you that this form has been used and is still widely used today by thousands of managers of all levels and brands all over the place, as I coached many of them and sold them on its merits.

Like most of the visuals/charts I used over the years, the dashboard or "managers' business plan" is just one page. Similar in a way to the one-page agents' business plan form I described in the previous chapter.

There are two main reasons why I kept on using the dashboard:

- On a single page, the plan numbers and the key variables that really matter jump off the page. Easy to catch, understand, correct or amend, if necessary, throughout the year
- The flow, from beginning to end, from the number of desks to the ROR (return on revenue) is logical. I'll explain a bit later and hopefully prove the point.

A business plan is very serious business. Especially of course for a manager. If you are at the helm, you are supposed to know what you are doing and where you are going. You must know your numbers, your market, your competitive advantages, or challenges. You are paid for your expertise.

A plan is not a wild guessing game or a bragging invitation. No BS. The company may depend on your projections to formulate its own; the same way that you need to take your agents' individual plans into account to draft your own.

To be totally honest, your company and others may decide to run a parallel plan for your office, just in case your numbers are not convincing. The CEO may be asked to take a good look at what your office did the year before, plug in some industry forecasts, cook up a couple of home-made analytics, and issue different conclusions and bottom-line numbers.

That does not excuse you from the responsibility to think hard and long about what you expect your performance to be though. You don't want upper management to think that your projections are ridiculous and you can't be taken seriously.

Dashboard form (See sample)

It takes agents to sell real estate. As such, the number of agents rightfully should be the starting point of any business plan.

Actually, as you will see on the sample form, I put the number of desks on the first line. I realize that you don't necessarily need desks to have agents but most offices do.

If you run a "traditional" real estate office with desks of some type, your first objective is to list more agents than you have desks for. As we said in another chapter (Space accommodations), some agents share desks and some agents don't need or deserve a desk.

Shoot, as a goal, for an occupancy factor of 125% or more to obtain the best results.

The next two lines are new to my standard form:

- *Hired* (number of new hires): How I forgot to mention this line to my first dashboard draft, I don't know. I stand corrected. The number of new hires, each and every month is a must on a projections chart. Hiring must be top of mind. If you do that well, that activity alone may

DASHBOARD

ABC Realty

Office: _____   Manager: _____   Year: _____

	January	February	March	April	May	June	July	August	September	October	November	December	TOTALS
Desks	88	88	88	88	88	88	88	88	88	88	88	88	88
Associates	110	107	107	104	105	106	106	106	106	107	107	107	107
Hired	0	0	2	0	1	3	1	0	2	3	1	1	14
Terminated	0	3	2	3	0	2	1	0	2	2	1	1	17
Listings	39	45	61	59	63	57	42	38	56	51	46	40	597
Open Sales	77	79	119	126	124	88	75	79	89	89	81	69	1095
% Closed to Open	90%	90%	90%	90%	90%	90%	90%	90%	90%	90%	90%	90%	90%
Closed Sales	69	71	107	113	112	79	68	71	80	80	73	62	985
Average Sales Price (000)	850	850	875	875	900	900	900	920	920	930	930	935	906,000
Closed Sales Volume (000000)	58.7	60.3	93.6	98.9	108	71.1	61.2	65.3	73.6	74.4	67.9	60	893,000,000
Commission %	2.5%	2.5%	2.5%	2.5%	2.5%	2.5%	2.5%	2.5%	2.5%	2.5%	2.5%	2.5%	2.5%
G.C.I (000)	1468	1508	2340	2472	2700	1778	1530	1640	1840	1860	1698	1500	22,325,000
% Retained	20%	20%	20%	20%	20%	20%	20%	20%	20%	20%	20%	20%	20%
Co. $ (000)	294	302	460	494	540	356	306	328	368	372	340	300	4,465,000
Oper. Exp. w/o Alloc. (000)	215	215	215	215	215	215	215	215	215	215	215	215	2,580,000
Allocation	0	0	0	0	0	0	0	0	0	0	0	0	0
Total Exp. w/Alloc. (000)	215	215	215	215	215	215	215	215	215	215	215	215	2,580,000
Operating Profit (000)	79	87	245	279	185	141	110	113	145	157	125	85	1,885,000
R.O.R													8.4%

solve many present or potential problems. As I wrote in the "recruiting" chapter, hiring agents is a never-ending job. An office is never full.

- *Terminated*: Yes, that's very much part of the job. No good reasons to keep undesirable associates (dead wood or bad attitude). Uphold your own production standards if you have any. Will only make good agents better and attract good producers from the competition.

The termination numbers can be misleading though. They could be a sign of weakness instead of strength. Most of the "terminated" are not shown the door, they leave of their own free will. When they are good, it is worrisome if not alarming. It is costly. The dollars lost may outweigh the dollars gained with the new recruits.

Next on the form: new listings. Huge. The number shows the strength of the office. If you have a lot of listings, you will almost always have a lot of sales: you can catch the buyers since you have what they look for, and you catch the attention of sellers looking for a strong office/company. You have something to advertise, brag about, and use as a bait to get more of the same. You control your destiny, so to speak.

The number of sales follows, logically. Sales of your own listings and those based on other brokers' listings.

Once you have the number of transactions and you have figured what your average price is likely to be, you arrive at a big number: the total dollar volume of sales, for each month, and for the year as a whole, all the way to the right of the form.

Then comes the commission rate. It obviously can/will vary based on your company's policy, on what other companies propose, on what you think you're worth and on the market conditions. Use your best educated guess.

Now you can find out the GCI (gross commission income).

Next, plug in what you foresee the Retained dollar percentage to be in order to get the precious Company Dollar, i.e. what the House gets to keep of the gross commission check you share with the agents.

The expenses need to be projected as well. The exercise is not too terribly hard though as most are pretty stable and therefore predictable. Dozens of items must be considered, including the three majors:

- Building/leases/equipment: the brick and mortar often takes the biggest chunk of your cashflow
- Salaries/payroll: you are a big part of it (hopefully)
- Advertising/marketing/promotion: can be heavy but it pays to spend the money
- Don't forget a possible allocation (franchise fee/royalties, etc.)

We finally made it to the end, the bottom-line, the anticipated operating profit. We all like the sound of it. I wish you a big one.

With this done, you can find out how good your performance will be if your plan is realistic. Divide the profit by the GCI and extract the ROR (return on revenue) percentage.

You are now done with your business plan. All that remains to be done is to actually deliver on it. Make it happen.

Key indicators

Hold on for another minute or two; there is one more thing I want to draw your attention to. There are four magic keys in your dashboard that you may want to play with to upgrade the quality of your numbers, to try to maximize your profit performance. Listen up:

- *The commission rate*: this one is a no brainer; if it goes up, so does your revenue. Can you do something about it? You bet. It's your money. It's your call on your own listings.

Up to you and the company to try to promote and uphold a rate that you think you deserve

- *The retained percentage*: don't give away the house when, more often than not, you don't have to. You are the boss, be fair but tough. Splits should be based on actual earnings, not promises or fairy tales. If you "buy" agents with unreasonable exceptions, you will be expected to do it again, and again

- *% closed to open sales*: not all sales can make it to closing and, in many cases, there is nothing you can do to keep the weak ones alive. However, if you and your agents are diligently staying on top of each transaction and act promptly on any potential danger, you can save/add lots of dollars to the bottom-line

- *Average sale price*: It can be what it is based on your market but it can also be what you wish it to be by focusing on the segment of the market you want to win. If your objective is to increase your market share at the high-end, your prospecting and marketing will need to be orchestrated and focused accordingly.

Chapter 14

MBO's – Management by Objectives

How do you measure and reward the success of your sales managers when you are running a large brokerage?

In most cases, the bottom-line profit tells the tale. If the office is in the black and shows respectable profit numbers for the year, the majority of real estate companies pay the office manager a performance bonus. The more profit you generate, the bigger the bonus, as the amount is often based on a percentage.

Generally speaking, I like bonuses. All managers do... When they get it. It's the carrot that keeps sales managers running.

There are, however, inherent flaws to a straight formula. Why? Because, in many instances, the manager has little if anything to do with the office good results. Sometimes the market conditions are sweet enough to blindly distribute incremental revenue/ profit to a bunch of companies and, consequently, to managers.

Sometimes, even though the manager is not an eagle or relaxes in the back seat, upper management is doing most of the driving.

That's why I am somewhat reserved on the effectiveness of a bonus which is not always deserved or which is paid irrespective as to whether or not the bottom-line profit exceeds expectations. It may very well reward the wrong guy for the wrong thing.

My preference has always been to reward managers based on what they do in relation to realistic goals, not just results. Goals formulated by the managers themselves (they own them) or, at least, goals agreed upon between managers and upper-management.

When pursued with diligence and determination, specific performance goals and the resulting bonus truly represent the quality of the manager and the focused efforts he/she needs to put forth to win the carrot.

Management by objectives (MBO's) goes beyond identifying goals and key results, it presents a quantifiable step by step guide to effective office management.

The MBO's program is composed of two distinct parts:

- *Quantity and accountability*: top business indicators deriving from business plan projections and comparative studies
- *Quality and attitude*: in a nutshell, the way to do the job in your company

The perfect format should fit the company's standard reporting methods and remove as much as possible, any and all areas of subjective evaluation. It should leave plenty of room for the manager's individual thinking and ingenuity.

I suggest that upper management sends the list of MBO's questions to the individual managers ahead of time so that they can review it carefully, familiarize themselves with the contents, and jot down their answers for each specific item.

The idea is or course to give them an extra bonus which will vary depending on how they perform in each area (upper management grade/prorate each one) and overall.

Example of MBO's questionnaire
MBO's meeting date:
Office:
Manager:

Words of wisdom

In the real estate business, managers have a pretty big ego. Most of them were previously top producers... with a big ego. Ego is a complex and fragile ingredient of the human mind. Sales managers generally don't appreciate being questioned about what they do and how they do it.

I – QUANTITY AND ACCOUNTABILITY

Reference: 2020 Business Plan (60% of the bonus)

A | SALES ASSOCIATES (20%)

1	RECRUITING (10%)
	▶ Number of new hires:
	▶ Who? (experienced vs. new):
2	RETENTION / TURNOVER (5%)
3	PRODUCTIVITY (SALES PER AGENT/Y) (5%)
	▶ Actual results vs. objectives

B | PRODUCTION (20%)

1	LISTING (5%)
	▶ Number of new listings:
	▶ Average price:
	▶ Share of primary market:
2	SALE (5%)
	▶ Number of sales:
	▶ Average price:
	▶ Share of primary market:
	▶ Number of in-house transactions:
3	GROSS VOLUME OF SALES (2%)
	▶ Actual result vs. objective:
	▶ Share of primary market:
4	GCI – GROSS COMMISSION INCOME (2%)
	▶ Actual result vs. objective:
	▶ % of Gross volume of sales:
5	COMPANY DOLLAR (3%)
	▶ Actual result vs. objective:
	▶ % of GCI – Retain %:
6	NET PROFIT (3%)

C | ROUTINE ACTIVITIES (20%)

1	OPEN HOUSES (10%)
	▶ Average number per week:
	▶ % of agents participating:
2	FARMING – GEOGRAPHIC OR SOI (5%)
	▶ Number of agents w. geographic farm(s):
	▶ Number of agents farming at least once/month:
	▶ % of homes in primary market:
3	PROSPECTING (5%)
	▶ Number of agents doing regular mailings:
	▶ Number of agents communicating w. prospects once/mo (email/texts, etc.):
	▶ Number of agents using social media:
	▶ Number of agents advertising in magazines or newspapers:

II – QUALITY AND ATTITUDE

Reference: 2020 Business Plan (40% of the bonus)

A	**COMPANY PROCEDURES AND POLICIES (10%)**

1	**ADHERENCE TO POLICIES (2%)**

▶ Manager listing and/or selling:

▶ Commission cutting:

▶ Commission split exceptions:

2	**PRINCIPLES/PHILOSOPHY (2%)**

▶ Soliciting agents from another home office:

▶ Agents listing/selling outside primary market:

3	**INTERACTION (2%)**

▶ Participation at managers' meeting:

▶ Participation at company meetings:

▶ Participation in company events, contests:

▶ Support of other managers:

▶ Legal issues:

4	**SUPPORT SYSTEM (2%)**

▶ Relocation:

▶ Use of company training:

▶ Use of legal assistance:

5	**INVOLVEMENT (2%)**

▶ Runs weekly sales meetings:

▶ Organizes in-office workshops or brainstorming sessions:

B	**MANAGEMENT SKILLS (10%)**

1	**EDUCATION, CLASSES/SEMINARS TO ATTEND (2%)**

▶ List of classes:

▶ Date for license renewal:

▶ Broker's license?

2	**PERFORMANCE REVIEWS (4%)**

▶ For agents (business plans, goals setting, minimum standards, etc.)

▶ For assistants (admin, IT, marketing):

3	**OFFICE RECOGNITION (4%)**

▶ Monthly program in place:

▶ Annual program in place:

C	**VISIBILITY (10%)**

1	**MANAGER'S INVOLVEMENT (5%)**

▶ Time in the office: ▶ Community events

▶ MLS tour: ▶ Charities:

2	**PROFESSIONAL ACTIVITIES (5%)**

▶ Local Board activity: ▶ Board sponsored events:

▶ Regional, state or national associations:

D	**IMPROVEMENT / ACTION PLAN (10%)**

1	**ACTIONS TO IMPROVE OFFICE PERFORMANCE (5%):**
2	**ACTIONS TO IMPROVE TEAM PERFORMANCE (5%):**

As a top executive, you may find that, even though they are routinely dealing with goals and expectations, some office managers have a hard time with accountability, especially when it means money. At the same time, it's only normal that upper management demands commitments and results.

With this in mind, I highly suggest you introduce the MBO's program in a very positive way. The company is not looking to reducing the manager' s income but looking at a way to increase it. It is a fabulous opportunity to qualify for a very juicy bonus (over and above any salary/override or other bonuses), based on actual results vs. agreed upon objectives.

How great a carrot is that? It's a win-win. The manager stands to add beaucoup dollars to his/her bank account and the company will add even more to the corporate cash register.

Chapter 15

SWOT Analysis

Who are we as an office, as a company, as a network?

Where do we stand within our competitive environment?

How can we win in our respective battlefields?

How do we go from "here," the present, to "there," the future, the objective?

What is our vision of who/what we want to become?

These are the right questions for managers or top real estate executives to ask themselves, and that they do.

The answers are a bit tougher to formulate.

Asking the right questions is a good beginning though. You don't need answers and you may not even know to think of answers if you don't have the right questions to begin with.

In business, the best way to think intelligently about both questions and answers is to do it in writing.

It is called SWOT: Strengths, Weaknesses, Opportunities, and Threats.

There is nothing a company can do which is more strategic in nature and more consequential in terms of conclusions, implementation and results.

The exercise starts with a self-assessment, whether you are managing an office, a group of offices or a company. You look both in the mirror and beyond the mirror, the surroundings.

You want to frame yourself within an objective context: the market where you operate among many competitors, and the conditions under which you and others have to work and try to succeed.

Individual and collective effort

You may or may not see a clear picture of the above. That's why

I recommend that, after you have done your part, you share your notes and compare them with that of other managers and, more importantly, with the executive(s) above you. It is a collective effort.

Upper management needs to know where you come from with your observations and ideas to better support you. They also need to look at the bigger picture and jot down their own observations and ideas to finetune the right vision for the company as such or the network.

To explain the process, I thought useful to fill in a typical SWOT analysis (see analysis) from a local company point of observation. On one side, how the company views itself and, on the other side (facing it), how the company views the network it is a part of.

Note: the proposed edits are only examples. The process, here, is more important than the contents. When you do your own SWOT, it's a different ballgame. Your notes must be pertinent.

The process is important but quite simple. As for the contents, they are of course primordial. They will determine your vision and the itinerary to follow to make it happen.

SWOT ANALYSIS

STRENGHTS

COMPANY: (identify)	NETWORK: (identify)
▶ Leadership position in X-county/region	▶ Third largest network in the country in dollar volume, 7th in number of transactions and 10th in number of agents
▶ Dominant market share in most local markets	
▶ Over 20% of the regional high-end market in both units and $volume	▶ Fastest growing network in the country over last three years
▶ Excellent name recognition	▶ Dominant market share of the relocation business in the US and internationally
▶ Strong local heritage/ background	
▶ Traditional full-service brokerage	▶ Several of the top companies in the country are part of the network
▶ Top notch associates with 6 in the national list of the best 500 agents	▶ Key alliances with strategic partners overseas
▶ Financially stable unit (as compared to a mostly fragmented and under-financed main competition)	

SWOT ANALYSIS

WEAKNESSES	
COMPANY: (identify)	**NETWORK: (identify)**
▶ Weak on technology tools	▶ Does not fit our image and style
▶ Relies too much on top producers	▶ Not a strong name in the state
▶ Half of the managers ready to retire	▶ The franchise fee eats up our profit
▶ Unclear identity and importance within the network	▶ Hybrid entity hard to describe and rely on
▶ Lack of communication and responsiveness from the network	▶ Do not seem to understand our needs and objectives
▶ "Us" vs. "they" syndrome between company and network	▶ We have never seen the network executives
▶ Confusion regarding who is supposed to do what between the company and the network	

SWOT ANALYSIS

OPPORTUNITIES

COMPANY: (identify)	NETWORK: (identify)
▶ In this slowing market, we should leverage our financial strength to go after top agents (or managers) from the competition ▶ Time to look at weak competitors for possible acquisitions or roll-ins ▶ Open the doors to more new agents to energize the troops and multiply prospecting opportunities ▶ Promote agents' advertising (subsidize?)	▶ Try to leverage the power of the network ▶ Good time to acquire strong regional companies in key US markets ▶ Should explore expanding into foreign markets (Europe? Asia?)

SWOT ANALYSIS

THREATS

COMPANY: (identify)	NETWORK: (identify)
▶ We are so good, we think we can do no wrong ▶ Complacency ▶ Progressively becoming administratively driven rather than sales driven ▶ Too many bosses to please ▶ Getting behind in technology ▶ Marketing team is too thin for the company's needs and the agents' demand ▶ Half of our offices need TLC ▶ We are not growing new managers to replace those about to retire	▶ Tendency to make decisions contrary to regional needs and interests ▶ Pushing new cookie-cutter national marketing programs which do not fit the sophistication of our regional make up ▶ Forcing offices/agents to use the network affinity partners

SWOT ANALYSIS

CONCLUSIONS / PRIORITIES	
COMPANY: (identify)	**NETWORK: (identify)**
▶ Focus on the company needs, as we see them ▶ Review and streamline our marketing tools ▶ Explore hiring consulting firm to drive traffic to our site ▶ Promote (subsidize?) agents' advertising ▶ Update our commission schedule ($ to achieve to move one level) to reflect rise in property values ▶ Implement "mandatory" technology training to bring all agents up to speed on new programs and software ▶ Identify managers' weaknesses and provide ad-hoc training classes ▶ Create a program to form potential new managers ▶ Ask services reps to visit offices at least every month to create more synergy	▶ Don't deal with all the network affiliates the same way as they are vastly different based on markets, size, performance, etc. ▶ Organize an annual convention to bring companies together and get both agents and managers to experience the power of the network ▶ Meet network top executives to pick their brains on how they see the future of real estate and how we fit in the picture

Chapter 16

Strategic Study & Plan

"Strategic," "Study," and "Plan", three big words in the real estate business lexicon. When used together, they sound so serious that they tend to make people nervous up and down the executive ladder.

All are awaiting the observations and conclusions of the SSP as if they were waiting for some kind of verdict, if not sentence. The day of reckoning if you will.

Well, let's relax and put things in perspective.

Real estate is a business, like any other. It has to be run as such. It is only good business, from time to time, to think hard and objectively about who we are as an organization in the context of an evolving competitive environment, and formulate grand objectives for the near and distant future.

Because it is sensitive, complex and can easily be biased, lots of companies which practice the sport choose to hire a consulting firm to do the job. Not sure it's a brilliant idea though as the consultants need to pick the brains of the top company players anyway to learn the market parameters in order to issue their recommendations.

I must confess that strategic studies are not my thing. Not any more to be precise. They used to be though. When I was a young real estate leader in search of perfection, I thought everything could be definitively explained and rationalized. I wrote a bunch of such studies. I would not waste too much time doing the same today.

The truth is, only ownership and/or the heads of a network, love the stuff and take the time to read it, because they are largely detached from the market action and need objective numbers and comments to judge a company's behavior in its environment.

Most other managers, whether office/sales managers or regional people, follow the market daily and know pretty well what they and their competitors are doing and where they are going.

A thorough strategic study encompasses a host of external economic variables:

- Economic forecast
- Business activity
- Competitive environment
- Employment picture
- Cost of mortgage money
- Political climate
- New developments, etc.

To save a few trees and a bunch of unnecessary pages on the above variables, I propose as a guide the following abbreviated version which focuses on internal factors as well as the regional market competitive environment. It is in fact a modified and shorter draft of a document I wrote many-many moons ago.

Strategic Study & Plan - ABC Realty – January 2020

I. Introduction

The following is not a formal strategic plan but a sampling of reflections and observations that will permit the leadership to establish a more thorough and final document.

As such, the choices, challenges and opportunities outlined in the text are merely the expression of a personal view based on my knowledge of the market/business and my understanding of the ownership's vision.

This is why the plan will need to be amended, completed, and validated to eventually represent a meaningful working document to be used as a reference and an itinerary for the growth of the company in the region, the state, the country, and internationally. Whatever applies.

II. Who are we today?

ABC Realty is the largest independent residential real estate company in X-State.

Over a short 6-year period, the company created a powerful network of 22 sales offices and approximately 650 sales associates, making it the fastest growing full-service brokerage in the state.

ABC Realty, with a total of 3,000 associates and 80 residential offices spread out in 5 states (list of states) is today the No.1 privately-owned real estate firm in all of the region (define the region) and the 15th largest real estate company in the US.

Always intent on riding the wave of innovation to best adapt to an ever-changing industry, ABC is an undisputed leader in the fields of technology and local, regional, national, and global marketing.

III. Who do we want to be?

- Key objective:

ABC wants to be the market leader or no less than the second best in all of the state local markets in which we have a sales office, with a minimum market share of 10% in each one.

ABC wants to be the leading force in full service real estate in the entire region.

ABC wants to be the leading reference in the "one stop shopping" concept, with strong ancillary business units in mortgage banking, Insurance, global relocation, and title services.

- Vision statement:

"To be the company of choice for the most discriminating buyers, sellers, associates and managers, and excel at providing all services related to a real estate transaction."

- Mission statement:

"Our sales associates are our partners. As an entrepreneurial private company, we partner with our sales associates to build their respective businesses and deliver quality services to all.

Together, we provide the most innovative and competitive real estate, mortgage, insurance, and settlement services."

IV. The market
- Scope:

We are today doing business in 22 different towns or districts which, together with their immediate surroundings, represent an aggregate population of approximately 800,000.

If we assume that, on average, 3 people live under the same roof, this would translate into about 240,000 households.

If we assume that 75% of the properties are owner occupied, this would translate into about 180,000 homes.

If we assume that homeowners, on average, stay in their home 10 years, this would translate into a potential of 18,000 sales per year.

If the objective is to account for 15% of all transactions within our regional marketplace, the bar is set at roughly 2,700 per year, or up to 5,400 sides.

This is our market potential.

- Landscape:

Our regional market stretches over nearly 200 miles. It is comprised of all that the state has to offer, from city life to suburbia and rural countryside. The towns where our offices are located vary in size from 1,500 residents (office name) to 100,000 (name). They vary just as much in terms of median price, going from $315,000 (average sales price) in X-Town to $1,500,000 (ASP) in Y-Town.

- The target:

There is only one thing that, with the possible exception of X-Town, our offices have in common: they all are located in affluent towns or villages. They are in "high-end markets." As such, they are not as likely to attract first time home buyers or investors or the majority of relocation transferees. On the other hand, they are more stable in terms of value and less prone to foreclosures.

- Market conditions:

The financial meltdown that shook up the industry over thirteen years ago still weighs heavily on the mind and the wallet. Although the dark days are over, real estate prices have hardly caught up with their highest levels. The domino effect of the crisis has affected more businesses, large and small, with all expected consequences in the employment sector, purchasing power, and a wait and see attitude from would-be buyers or sellers.

It must be noted that the company has fared relatively well in the downturn in relation to its competitors and the market as a whole, and the momentum has accelerated regularly during the recovery years and to this day.

Last year, between January 1 and May 13, the company, according to the MLS, sold 506 homes in the state (6.8% more than in 2018) for $280,230,683 (17.75% more than in 18). This is to be compared to the overall market stats: over the same 41/2 months of 2019, 8,409 homes sold in the state (5.5% more than in 18).

We are now number 3 in the state in terms of volume of sales behind company1 and company2 (by a split of a hair). We were # 4 at the same time in 2017.

Same photo at the listing end: ABC was number 4 in the first 41/2 months of 2018 with 1.8% of the listing units and this year, we are #2 with a market share of 2.8%.

More remarkable is the fact that our listing inventory over this period of time shows an increase of 7.2%, while the listings are down 21.2% in the state, all companies combined.

We are beating the market and establishing momentum. This, combined with low mortgage rates and abundant money being made available to more prospective buyers, represents a good omen for the firm's second half performance.

- Market focus/positioning:

Our biggest challenge...But also our best opportunity. We are working on it.

- *Primary market*:

Today, we have a shotgun approach to the market. We are chasing listings and sales all over the map. The fraction of the business we actually do in our primary markets (towns in which our offices are located + adjacent towns where ABC has no physical presence) is surprisingly weak.

In any local market, only the top three firms/offices with a minimum of 10% market share are clearly identified with the town; they belong there.

If, for the first 41/2 months, we use this bar as a reference, we are among the players that count in only three towns: X-Town (#1 w. 31.7% share), Y-Town (#1 w. 25% share) and Z-Town (#2 w. 13.5% share).

Accordingly, those offices show the highest or the second highest average sales price in their town. Two of our offices are in the #3 spot in their respective town (names); all the others range between the #4 and #7 spot with market shares as low as 3.2%.

We produce "accidental" business. This unpredictable situation is not sustainable. The primary market is our battlefield. That's where we are judged by both the principals and the competition. That's, ultimately, where we have to win.

Getting business elsewhere is great short term because it pays the bills but, on an on-going basis, it is pushing our agents to distant lands that we have no interest in harvesting and where we/they might get lost.

We must refocus the bulk of our activity on the respective primary markets to create recurring business and grow market share substantially. The action steps are obvious:

a. *Open houses:* The more the better but with a "local" focus. The goal is to reach a 90% agents' participation over the weekend (Sunday & Saturday) or 65% just on Sunday. No matter what, no matter where, the participation should never be below 50% of the agents. Under the 50% mark, we can only trade water.

b. *SOIs:* First and foremost, we need to cover our primary markets like a blanket with mailings (work on various types at next managers' meeting).

c. *Recruiting:* Same priority, we need local soldiers, those who can best benefit from our local presence and those from whom we can most benefit. If they are part of the local life with personal networks or affinity groups, we are going to make our job easier of growing smoothly and organically. Everybody wins.

d. *Advertising:* Same as above. The properties featured in our display ads should be chosen according to the following 2 priorities: 1) local homes, 2) high-end properties.

- *High-end business:*

To the extent that, as we have said earlier, our offices are located in high-end communities but we account for a modest part of such primary markets, we do not play a major role at the high-end at this point.

In most areas, our average selling price tells the story: we are lagging behind several competitors. This prevents us from identifying with the segment of the market which is essential to our growth. In a way, we dress for the part but we don't play it. That will change.

- *In-house sales:*

You show me those offices in any town which have the largest percentage of in-house sales and I'll show you the leading offices. That's true of the big guns like company1 which can dominate in this department since they have more listings to work with, but it is also true of smaller firms/offices which work and leverage their inventory harder.

In order to improve our record, we are now establishing a 3-step protocol in the offices which works as follows:

1. The listing agent, immediately upon taking the listing or even earlier if it is a sure thing, should broadcast the info (address, price, showing instructions...) to all local/ regional ABC associates to crank up the engine.

2. We have one full day to place a listing in the MLS, meaning that if we take a listing on Monday morning, we don't have to shoot it to the MLS before Tuesday, thereby giving plenty of time to our agents to have a 24 hours + free ride. The goal is to reach a 10 to 15% in-house sales in every office. That, in itself, can produce at least 5% incremental business and income for the firm, the office and of course for the associates.

3. All local ABC agents should make a point of rushing to the new company listings to preview them (and eventually show them) instead of waiting until the office weekly tour day or the MLS tour day just because "it is more convenient".

V. The competition

For the most part, they are the same brands doing the same things with the same bells and whistles from one coast to the next. The main categories are:

1. The national franchises: they are today suffering more than the other players. They are commodities used by investors to produce as big a return as possible. When the real estate business is good, everybody is dancing; when the business is cold and the investors are done squeezing the lemon, then what? As I was nasty enough to suggest once, investors thought these firms were cash cows, but

when the cash is gone, what do you do with the cows.

2. The discount brokers who have to cut commissions as they don't have anything else to cut. They are like mosquitoes: we know that at the end of Summer they may largely be gone but, in the meantime, they sting pretty good and it hurts.

3. The low cost/low fat cafeteria Realtors: You pay as you go. Amazingly enough, many sellers fall for it.

4. The large independent, regional and full-service companies, including our own: they are today in a unique position to take over many markets. They know how to use their network of offices to create synergy. They depend only on themselves and can cater their services to attract the best agents, respond to the clients' needs, and adapt quickly to market conditions.

5. There is actually another type of "competitor": we'll cover the profile in the "paradigm" section.

We need to review carefully the strengths and weaknesses of each one of the main competitors in each one of the above categories in order to exploit their Achilles tendon.

I suggest that, whenever possible at the regional level (Productivity meetings?), we get all managers involved in the SWOT exercise.

SWOT *(See separate chapter elsewhere in the book)*
Strengths:
- Privately owned
- Independent
- Financially stable
- State of the art technology
- Visionary leader
- Excellent managers
- Agents' loyalty

- Entrepreneurial with can do attitude
- High-end image
- Elegant and welcoming offices
- Good looking sign
- Great mortgage unit
- Great relocation services

Weaknesses:

- Second class syndrome in the state
- Lack of common culture
- Challenging communication between offices and the corporate office
- New training format for new licensees
- Perception that we charge too many fees

Regarding Threats and Opportunities, I suggest that we involve all managers in this exercise that can best be accomplished in a relaxed brainstorming session.

VII. The Paradigm

We are no longer the only active actor in the real estate business. Traditional companies are challenged and menaced.

The internet changed the rules long ago. It created a bypassed connection to buyers and sellers.

Internet aggregators, syndicated sites and technology-minded real estate companies are trying to bring both the supply and the demand to their own "fishbowl" to try to control the connections, the relationships, and eventual transactions.

Real estate companies/offices are no longer the first point of contact for buyers looking for a home or sellers looking to sell one.

We need to evolve in the "life style" business to drive and keep our clients on our site. Our advertising strategy should be to direct the traffic to our brand.

It will be our challenge to progressively share the print

media advertising responsibility with the agents who can best benefit from a self-promotion which leverages the firm's and the offices' strengths. The process in on-going and is spreading rapidly.

VIII. Sales managers

Are the present managers the right ones? They probably are, at least for now and a foreseeable future that we have only so much control over. We have a great team of office leaders, competent, devoted and loyal. Now we need to build a bench because today, it's pretty thin. We are trying to identify possible managers in and outside the house.

The objective is to find tigers among the competitors' ranks with enough influence that they could come on board together with lots of top notch associates.

Here is a brief assessment of the managers we now have.

(See chapter 8 "Office sales managers' checkup")

IX. Key challenges & recommendations

• The shape of growth:

Horizontal, with more offices spread out on the map, or vertical: keeping the network pretty much as it is but maximizing productivity and resulting net profit? Both?

Regarding the opening of new offices, we might want to identify on a map the most logical locations, those which are in harmony with the high-end image we need to promote to facilitate growth.

In terms of productivity improvement, we have to depend mostly on the managers' abilities and commitments, but we also need to better leverage our training/coaching team.

Today, most of our managers are good at promoting and monitoring activities (SOIs, open houses, etc.) but they need to do more than that to be effective managers accountable for the profit of their branch.

- Franchises:

Idea to further explore. Great revenue opportunity which can also grow the brand. Particularly useful in communities far removed from our stronghold. Challenge: making sure that the franchisees carry the image of ABC, abide by the rules, and use the same or similar branded or co-branded marketing tools.

- Acquisitions/Joint ventures:

Cheapest way to grow, if the candidates fit the mold, if the price is right and, of course, if the agents stay put. If nothing else, the market is pretty good for this option. Quite a sport though to find the right candidates and get them to play ball.

- Size of offices:

Perhaps the biggest challenge. Are our existing offices compatible with our growth expectations and the evolution of the industry?

Most are around 3,000 sqft. and house about 30-40 associates. In a good market when sales are coming in big numbers, it is a comfortable size/population. However, when the market is dry, it may be exactly the wrong size: too big or too small.

Considering that the operating expenses are almost fixed and that the expenses delta between a medium size office and a larger one is not that big, it is obvious that we should opt for large capacity offices. It takes 40 people on average to break even and, over that, it is almost pure profit.

- Action steps:

1. Get the office population to full desk capacity with only active agents. In the majority of our offices, we are not there yet. We have a lot of dead wood.

2. Fine-tune the team to progressively upgrade the level and the performance of each office (managers, regionals, general manager)

3. Go over desk capacity. Use the "Effective Desk Occupancy" chart to optimize the revenue that each desk should bring. The idea is to look at each desk as an individual profit center (See separate chapter on the subject).

4. What office size and layout do we need for tomorrow's business? Workstations instead of desks? Cafe-type relaxed layout? A living room atmosphere with only a few desks and a couple of conference rooms to conduct business? Choices are many. Set up a small committee (managers and upper management) to study options.

Chapter 17

Acquisitions and Roll-ins

The first short-term objective of most small real estate brokerages is to survive, pay the bills, and try to secure a little profit here and there to buy another year or more (or less). Short of succeeding at playing wise squirrels, there is no long-term objective to worry about.

Powerful large real estate organizations, whether independent, affiliated to a network, or networks themselves, have to deal with a different set of challenges. Money, they already have. The question is "what can we do with it to keep it coming?"

So goes the real estate industry. Opposite views and ambitions reflect opposite existential realities.

If you allow me to generalize a little to make a point, I will say that to stay alive and have a chance to remain financially viable in this industry, you have a choice to make:

- Choose, deliberately, to be small, or
- Choose to get even bigger
- Anything in between is hazardous for your health

If you are very small, you can do all right. There are quite a few agents, turned brokers, who are totally satisfied leveraging their past clients and their sphere of influence as they get enough listings and sales to enjoy a good life. From a hole in the wall, in any given local market, you can enjoy a nice little niche if you keep your expenses as low as your ambitions.

If you are big and successful, your challenge is to remain big and successful. To protect your leadership position in whatever marketplace where you operate, you have to try to grow even more. Strong competitors are waiting in line, closely watching your moves. You grow or you shrink, there is no status quo.

Big fish syndrome

There are many ways to grow, each one with its own opportunities and risks:

As a CEO or an owner, you can burn cash (your own or that of a bank) to expand geographically in or close to your regional stronghold. One office at a time. Somewhat logical. If, as a powerful brand, you are known to do well in your existing market, chances are you will not have too much of a challenge exporting your success next door.

When the expansion market is similar in terms of price and prestige, you may be welcome as an already strong and well-respected player. You belong there.

If the new turf is more affordable than the one you come from, it is even easier. Local buyers and sellers probably know your company name and may identify it with high-end DNA and success.

That's the beauty of a "feeder market." Not only can you use your reputation to harvest a lot of new listings in the more affordable neighboring town(s), but you can attract local buyers in a move-up mode to your core market.

This "organic" option is great. It is natural and usually successful. It used to be THE way to grow in the 70's and 80's. That's when many of the leading regional companies built their empires.

There is one "problem" though: it takes time. Too much time at a time when time is money. Investors and shareholders don't like to wait, when they smell opportunities, they jump.

As a CEO/president of a company or a network, you can save yourself a lot of precious time by going the acquisitions route. A bit more risky to be sure but, if the reconnaissance work and the diligence process are properly thought through and managed, it is the preferred way to get from big to bigger and from bigger to huge.

When you are a big fish, you get to choose your prey. If you are lucky, the prey may very well initiate the inquiry.

The geographic scope of such option has virtually no limits. Acquisitions may take place within a region or a state but the hunting grounds may also cover the entire country and even reach foreign lands.

Acquisitions are sometimes called mergers. It's a nice word, a considerate way to flatter the ego of the lesser of the two companies and, in so doing, prevent or reduce the risk of turning off the proud agents who stand to change business cards.

Rarely are acquisitions a marriage of equals. The strength of either company is not based on the number of offices, or agents or even transactions, the strength or either company is based on bottom-line numbers. Money talks.

The real estate landscape has considerably changed over the last twenty years and the pace of change has brutally accelerated in recent years with well-funded hybrid real estate firms absorbing privately owned leading regional brokerages right and left.

Nothing, it seems, can prevent wealthy individuals or business entities to use their money to play in the real estate arena. Oh well.

Since we are talking big numbers here, it is obvious that the decision makers are the companies' leaders and the deals are so confidential and fragile that mum is the word. Sales managers of all levels are not in the know, unless it is indispensable to seek their advice on markets, offices, managers and top producers.

How does it work?

An acquisition, whatever the product or the service, is based on an agreed price. In our industry, the price is based on a tangible number/value, more or less inflated depending on how badly you want to buy or to sell.

The tangible number is called EBITDAR, for Earnings Before

Interest, Tax, Depreciation, Amortization & Royalty.

The price is calculated in multiples of EBITDAR. Other factors can cause multiples to fluctuate greatly, the biggest one being the state of the economy and what it does to the relative value of a company. How is the targeted company likely to fare in a downturn, or a boom?

Typically, the acquisition price varies between 2 and 6 times EBITDAR, with the scale arrow moving up or down in accordance with the size of the target. As such, a company with a $300M GCI is likely to be valued at 4 or 5 times EBITDAR.

Let's look closer at what the numbers could look like for a targeted company:

Total GCI last 12 months (LTM):	$100,000,000
Agents' share of the commission dollars:	$ 80,000,000
Co$:	$ 20,000,000
Total operating expenses:	$ 15,000,000
EBITDAR:	$ 5,000,000
Possible price:	$ 25,000,000

Adjustments can and will be made during the diligence process. They may concern upper management compensation depending on whether or not key executives stay on board.

Gains for the sale of assets and closed offices may also be considered in the final price.

Chocolate soufflé

I have been involved in a number of significant acquisitions and, if there is something that I learned from the experience, it is that the making of an acquisition strangely resembles the making of a chocolate souffle...

If you know a little bit about a chocolate soufflé, you probably know that it is incredibly difficult to dose ingredients and carefully control temperatures as well as cooking time such that the souffle succeeds at getting its signature height right before serving.

I guarantee that preparation and process are similarly very delicate in an acquisition.

Just like when you remove the souffle from the stove with an accelerated heartbeat in fear that it might collapse, a similar scenario can happen when you deliver the big news about the acquisition to the troops (managers and associates). The last step can prove to be the arduous and most consequential.

It is also the one which is often underestimated and underprepared.

What to look for

What is it that justifies the price and guarantee the value of an acquisition? What is the company actually buying?

It's not the offices. Some may actually need to be closed as they do not fit the needs.

It's not the furniture and the equipment. Easy enough to replace.

What the company is "buying" is the sales team, the agents who sell the real estate and the managers who keep them busy and successful. Together they produce the results that the acquisition price is based on.

If the agents and the managers stay, the souffléis beautiful. If they don't, the company wasted its money.

Hence the need to bring the general sales manager and regional managers in the loop slightly ahead of time. They must share their thoughts about the communication process, how to present the acquisition as a big win for everyone, with as many perks and pluses as possible.

Office managers must feel their job is secure and the future better than the past so that, in turn, they convey the good news with enthusiasm to the agents, commencing with the top producers.

Too often, the "after the acquisition" phase is neglected. Managers and agents are left in the dark. When the CEO breaks the news to the troops at a general meeting called at the last minute, people are naturally surprised, if not shocked. Pretty hard to control a surprise. It can go in any direction. There is no safe gamble.

Roll-ins

There is another way, a low key and mostly "friendly" way to acquire another company. I am talking about what we refer to as "roll-ins."

Roll-ins, for the most part, involve smaller competitors who happen to either be located in possible expansion areas targeted by the bigger fish or are located in the same market(s) but would add significant market share and strength to the company.

In either case, the "merger" must make sense to both sides. One takes over a competitor's business and salesforce, and the other no longer needs to worry about sometimes worrisome financial hurdles. It's a win-win.

The two sales teams are getting something out of it: added fire power for some and security and more tools and services for the others.

There is little risk that agents and/or managers will object to the change as it is explained by the respective brokers themselves, leaders that agents and managers of smaller companies usually love and respect.

How it works

Placing a value, a price, on a real estate company considered for a roll-in is difficult. Its most important assets are intangible:

- The agents are independent contractors
- Their reputation
- Their inventory of listings and what is in the pipeline

- The goodwill of the brokerage

The real value is not so much what the targeted company has today as it is its future revenue stream. As the roll-in name suggests, it is expected that most agents (and possible management) will remain with the buying company.

The broker-owner often joins as well, as a selling office manager. This is the ideal scenario, a quick and pain free transition. One office rolls smoothly into another. Hence the name.

Formula for payout with owner on board

- I like something along the following lines:
- A "small" amount of cash upfront (includes furniture and equipment) to grease the deal
- Owner receives an 80% lifetime split on his/her personal production
- Owner keeps 100% of the revenue on office sales already in the pipeline
- Owner receives 10% override on the company dollar generated by "his/her" transferred sales associates during the first year and 5% during the second year (retention tactic)
- Owner receives a 50% referral fee on the Co$ generated by all listings transferred to the buying company if such listings go into contract within six months, or a 25% fee after that

If the owner chooses to leave, the roll-in modalities can be similar to that of an acquisition.

In that case, a letter of confidentiality is necessary and the selling broker must fill out an "Acquisition information checklist" to corroborate the price.

This detailed document usually covers at least three years and includes, at a minimum:

- Number of offices, number of desks, number of agents and number of salaried employees (managers and staff)
- Number of closed transactions, closed volume of sales, closed sales units, gross commission rate, GCI, retaining percentage, Company dollar
- Pending transactions as of ...
- Operating expenses, operating profit
- Listings inventory as of...
- Company legal status, ownership interest
- List of all employees, with titles, duties and salaries
- List of all agents, with present splits
- Breakdown of revenues between residential sales, commercial, property management
- Schedule of services offered to agents or principals
- Breakdown of who pays for expenses such as E&O, cards, signs, phone, MLS, advertising and prospecting tools...
- Financial statements with balance sheet, income statements, year to date income
- List of fixed assets, copy of leases and pending transactions
- Copy of the commission schedule
-

Sounds like a lot but, let's face it, any respectable company, small or large, should keep all such documents at hand or available on short notice. That's a business after all.

Chapter 18

Market Targets – What, Where, Why

Real estate is a local business. You heard that many times, right? But what are you doing, as a manager, to identify your local/ primary market and try to concentrate your hunting within its boundaries?

You may say "who cares where my associates get their listings and make the sales, commission dollars are based on price and the office gets its commission regardless whether the property is located in the local market or in Timbuktu."

I know. I get it. But bear with me. I have a point to make.

Please answer the following questions:

- If your local turf is in a small county of, say, California, how many transactions do you expect to make in Timbuktu? Do you agree with me that this kind of deals is more the exception than the rule? An accident of sort?
- If you do get a listing or a sale far away from your small county, do you really think that the neighbors are going to make the connection between this transaction and your office located far away? Do you really think that if they decide to sell or buy another home close to the present one, they will trust you to handle both deals, or even just one?
- If these people are indeed from another planet and, against all odds and common sense, want your agent to list their home, what exactly do you plan on doing to properly market the Timbuktu house? Weekend open houses until it sells? Burning lots of dollars advertising in the local papers?
- If more of the neighbors are intrigued about whether your

125

agent got lost in a foreign territory but nevertheless solicit your agent's services to list or buy, are you prepared to open an office in Timbuktu to harvest this miraculous mushrooming business?

OK, you probably got my point. It does not pay great rewards to work far away from home. In fact, it is risky as it takes your agents' time, their/your money, and especially their/your focus away from where they/you are most likely to shine and obtain the best results: the local market.

The local market is the market you know best. It is where most of your agents work and reside. It is where you are most recognized and judged as a real estate entity, by homeowners, potential buyers, and other brokers/agents.

The local market, because of the above, is where you can create recurring business. If you get a listing and you plant your local sign in front of the house, you are likely to get more of the same. And the buyers, in time, will call on you again when they decide to move.

That's how you grow your business, one local listing or sale at a time. That's how you get your marketing money's worth and how your agents can best leverage their time, whether on open house, prospecting or showing property.

That's how you build your local market share and become (or remain) relevant as a major player. In my book, an open house in the primary market is worth five open houses elsewhere.

Today, it is very easy to track where, when and what you do in the way of business. The MLS, for the most part, does it for you, daily, monthly, and for whatever year you want to check. It compares your local activity to that of other companies and/or agents, and from one month or one year to the next.

Pretty nice, really, especially if you run a small outfit with little in the way of financial means. Now you have the tools to play Realtor, just like the big companies and networks. In a way it's not fair to them because it is leveling the field, but I am not going to cry over that today.

Let's go back to square one: since you, as a company or as an office, you have the tools to measure the quantity and the quality of your business in your local market, do you actually do it? Do you use the geographic data to drive your agents' activities such that you and they can keep on growing? Do you integrate the data in your business plan and key objectives?

Market penetration study

As much as I like to play with the MLS to know where I stand, at any given time in the real estate universe, I have to confess that my favorite visual to get a clear picture of what an office/company does in the market, is a form called "Market Penetration Study" that I devised many decades ago when I ran a 20+agents office brokerage.

This form, which I used through the years irrespective of the flag I happened to represent, made it very simple to follow, at a glance, my performance through the months against the competitors and the local MLS.

Check it out. You might decide to play with it and make it your own market visual.

(See partially completed Market Penetration Study chart)

Primary market

The first thing that you have to do, as a manager using the form, is define your primary market:

- The town where your office is located (or district of a large city)
- The towns adjacent or in near proximity to yours (typically 3 to 6)

Each town, commencing with yours as #1 (local market), is designated at the bottom of the form (#1, #2, #3, #4, #5)

All other towns are thrown into the "other" box.

MARKET PENETRATION STUDY

ABC Realty

Office: 1 - Local Office   Manager: _____   Month/Year: April/2020

LISTINGS, AS PER MLS

ABC REALTY OFFICES AND COMPETITORS' OFFICES	# OF UNITS LISTED		% OF UNITS LISTED		$ VOLUME OF LISTINGS		AVERAGE PRICE	
	CM	YTD	CM	YTD	CM	YTD	CM	YTD
ABC 1 - Local	18	90	10%	10%	15.3M	76.5M	850K	850K
ABC 2	6	30						
ABC 3	2	10						
TOTAL ABC	26	130	14.4%	14.4%				
COMPETITOR #1 Name - Local	23	115	13%	13%	21.9M	86.3M	795K	750K
COMPETITOR #2 Name - Local	12	60						
COMPETITOR #3 Name - Local	6	30						
MLS REGION	180	900	100%	100%			100%	

CLOSED SALES, AS PER MLS

ABC REALTY OFFICES AND COMPETITORS' OFFICES	# OF UNITS SOLD		% OF UNITS SOLD		$ VOLUME SOLD		AVERAGE PRICE	
	CM	YTD	CM	YTD	CM	YTD	CM	YTD
ABC 1 - Local	39	170	10.3%	11.3%	30.4M	133M	780K	782K
ABC 2	17	80						
ABC 3	5	8						
TOTAL ABC	61	258	16%	17.2%				
COMPETITOR #1 Name - Local	55	225	14.5%	15%	39.1M	155.2M	710K	690K
COMPETITOR #2 Name - Local								
COMPETITOR #3 Name - Local								
MLS REGION	380	1500	100%	100%			100%	100%

CURRENT MONTH LISTINGS BY TOWN (MLS)

TOWNS	#1 Name	#2 Name	#3 Name	#4 Name	#5 Name	OTHER
ABC TOTALs	8	6	4	4	0	0
YTD TOTALS	40	30	20	20	8	2

CURRENT MONTH SALES BY TOWN (MLS)

TOWNS	#1 Name	#2 Name	#3 Name	#4 Name	#5 Name	OTHER
ABC TOTALs	36	20	10	0	0	0
YTD TOTALS	200	82	49	21	5	

It goes without saying that, ideally, you want your office to perform best in the town where your office is located and hopefully better than another office of the same brand located in a different town.

If the market penetration study shows that the "local" office (X1 on the form) gets less listings or less sales in their own local market than other offices of the same company, there is something wrong with the picture. The manager and/or upper management has some work to do, to say the least. Who needs a "local" office if another distant office of the brand has more transactions in its local turf?

Competition

In the first column, you list your office first, then, if and when relevant, other company offices.

Your main competitors will follow.

At the bottom of the section, you list the MLS region that you and your competitors are a part of.

Obviously, this will tell you what your office does in relation to not only other offices of the same brand but other local offices you compete with at both the listing end and the sale end:

- Every month (units and % share of the MLS total)
- Year-to-date (same as above)
- Dollar volume of listings or sales for the month and year to date
- The average price of listings and sales, by month and year to date

This last indicator, the average listing price and average sales price, has always been a big eye opener for me as my focus is the high-end business. Everything being equal in the way of commission rate, it pays ten times more to sell a $5 million home as it does to sell ten at $500k a piece. And it's not necessarily harder, contrary to what most people think. Different mindset and different tools mostly, that's all.

If your goal is to win the high-end battle in your local market but your average listing price and your average sales price are lagging behind that of one or more competitors, you better think long and hard about what magic to put in place ASAP to solve the problem. Or you can forget about the dream and accept to live as best you can with the reality.

My motto has always been: if I get the big ones (especially listings), I can get all the others. The others come more easily as most sellers want to do business with reputable offices/companies/agents who have the trust of the fortunate few wealthy sellers and buyers.

People who know how to make lots of money are usually pretty good at making the right business decisions. How can you argue about their judgement when it comes to choosing a Realtor?

Enough said on the subject, I don't like to talk about money ☺.

You might want to share the "Market Penetration Study" form with some of your key associates to help them better understand the value of targeting the market with a rifle rather than with a shogun.

Many, if not most agents are running after too many rabbits in too many areas. "Cold callers" particularly are soliciting business all over the place in search of another deal and another opportunity to get a check.

It's a dangerous game. For one thing those agents may not know anything about values, market conditions or advertising venues in a "foreign" market. To make matters worse, they often represent themselves wrongly as "local experts" associated with the "local office" which, if it is not true, is fraud.

It's OK for agents to expand their hunting grounds. They have to make a living. But, as a manager, you better explain to them the limits of what they can do and say as to avoid lawsuits and run a nice and thriving profit center.

Chapter 19

High-End Focus

Allow me to talk about my favorite topic, the luxury market, and, at the same time, help real estate managers of all levels out there understand the strategic and financially rewarding value of focusing on the high-end.

Since the high-end business has been my DNA throughout my professional life, I just felt compelled to write a chapter on this segment of the market neglected too often by too many brokers.

In this fiercely competitive business, you have two basic and objective ways to assess and compare real estate companies, offices and even agents, aside from looking at the bottom line profit or a bank account balance:

- You can choose to look at the total number of transactions, or
- You can look at your total $ sales volume

At the end of the day, both numbers may deliver the same revenues but one number focuses on quantity, while the other focuses on quality. Big difference today, and a likely bigger one tomorrow, if you fail to recognize which one matters most.

I don't know about you but, even though I am dazzled at the hundreds of deals some super-agents can close in a year, I am more impressed by those agents who achieve the same financial results or better in a fraction of the time thanks to a much higher average sales price.

As you well know, there is only so much you can do as a company or a sales associate to create more sales, especially when listings are scarce or in a down-market. Tough to increase revenues and volume market share if you are not a player at the high-end.

The high-end is often the market driver, the locomotive that signals a recovery, and eventually pulls the rest of the wagons. In any region, state, or even country. No surprise that the top companies and agents are almost always those which dominate the high-end. These brokers have the trust of the affluent sellers. They can leverage that reputation to collect trophy listings and attract more sellers in all price ranges.

That's the beauty of a successful high-end record: not only does it not affect negatively your ability to get the bread and butter sales but it actually increases the opportunity for more of those sales as most home sellers would want to list their homes with the company and the agent who listed Mr. Rockefeller's property. They are wanted.

As I like to say: when you have the big ones, it's a heck of a lot easier to get the others. The shiny high-end image acts as a magnet. Everybody would like to identify with it.

Again, the only number that counts is the end result, denominated in dollars. If you spend little time achieving great success, so much the better. Good for you and my hat to you.

As an agent, ask yourself this question: would you rather sell 100 homes at $300,000 or just 10 at $3M?

It's not just about the money, which may be the same. It's about the glory, the prestige, the feeling that you belong to the elite. You are a member of a very exclusive club. You "made it" in the business. You are the local hero that both sellers and other Realtors are looking up to.

As a company leader, recognizing that you may need to raise your average sales price to improve your bottom line, how can you gravitate your way to the juicy but elusive luxury market and seduce top high-end agents?

It starts with you, as a company leader. It's all about who you are, who you want to be when you grow up, and what you can do about it. Gutsy move. Tough strategic changes have to be made. You can't do business as usual if you are not satisfied with the results you are getting and those you anticipate.

Think big. I admire brokers who always challenge themselves to do a little bit better what they already do well, but I have a lot more admiration for those visionaries who dare to change their focus and strategy to win and thrive in their marketplace. That's what a high-end program can do for any brokerage.

Let's brainstorm a bit about a few thoughts and tips on how to crack the high-end door open and eventually cut yourself a nice slice of the luxury market:

- *Use your competitive advantages*

To begin with, do you actually know what you have, within your company or within the network, that represents significant differentiators you can leverage to get a bigger piece of the action at the high-end?

What is special and unique about you, as a company, as an office, as an agent? What makes you different and better than the other guys? Everybody is the best at something. Is that something susceptible of helping you get a high-end listing?

What can the name, the tools, the services, and the overall power of your company and whatever network you are a part of do to help you win in the luxury market?

I traveled extensively on the world map and got to talk with thousands of real estate pros about this very question. Interestingly enough, I found that most of the pros don't really know their own competitive advantages.

I remember one meeting I attended in Los Altos, many-many moons ago, when I was running a large multi-offices company. I asked the manager and the associates to identify what they perceived to be notable competitive advantages. They all went blank. They had no clue. Not one answer, just perplexed faces. I swear it was not just my French accent.

Then I started teasing them with a few pointers to open and challenge their minds. Eureka, a few answers started spurting from the aisles, followed by waves of others.

Believe it or not, about half an hour later, I jotted down exactly 100 benefits of association on the board! Everyone felt so proud and so fortunate to have so many distinctive advantages over the competition. The exercise proved to be so amazing that I used the magic recipe many times over the years.

Might want to put the idea to the test to help jump-start a high-end program.

- *High-end marketing program*

If you want to become a force at the high-end, you need to start by defining the vision and developing an impressive and credible specialized marketing program.

Your high-end marketing program must address both the needs of the sellers of luxury homes, the needs of those buyers who are qualified, and potentially interested in purchasing them, and the needs of the agents who want to move up in the world.

As a Realtor, you are the communication vector between the supply and the demand. When you have one side, you have to look for the other. You need to bridge the gap between the two, get them to connect through marketing, advertising, and all means of promotion.

- *You cannot market extraordinary homes with ordinary means*

Every luxury home is unique. The marketing vehicles, whether in print or online, need to be tailored to each property.

Keep in mind that producing a flyer, a brochure, a video tour, a social media campaign, or whatever else, is not enough and may in fact be irrelevant if your marketing does not reach the audience you need to target.

As an example, it's a farce to suggest that online marketing reaches wealthy Chinese buyers on the main land when everybody knows (or should know) that the message cannot bypass the internet Great Firewall.

- *Remember that at the high-end, the job is not merely to list a home, it's to get it sold*

Our ability to list (and especially to keep on listing) is usually predicated on our ability to sell. Too often, agents focus on winning a trophy listing and depend on others to finish the work. They think that have accomplished their mission once they get a signature on a listing agreement. They relax and start counting their commission dollars.

Well, all they have done at that point is one part of the job, only the beginning. Listing is merely an invitation to do the job. What really matters comes next.

I guaranty that a seller has a very different understanding of the mission he/she is entrusting the agent with. His/her objective is not to list the property, it is to find a buyer and sell the house. That's what a seller hires us for.

- *While luxury properties are local, the likely buyers may not be*

Again, can your marketing arrows reach out to potential buyers in other regions and countries? Do you have a global dimension you can use, whether through your company or international networks?

Size matters. As an isolated office or a small local company, you just don't have the means of marketing effectively a multi-million dollar listing beyond regional boundaries.

You need to belong to and leverage the power and the marketing dimension of an organization which has the name recognition and the tools/services which are required to get the job done countrywide and internationally.

- *Dress for the part*

If you want to be a major player at the high-end, you not only have to dress for the part with an impressive marketing program, but you also need to play the part. They actually need to use the program. Hello?

Your agents are an extension of the company. They represent it. They need to identify with the high-end and systematically use the company program to open doors and close the deal. They also may need to modify their personal advertising image accordingly to create the right perception.

- *Marketing and selling a luxury home is a team effort*

An agent, alone, cannot properly market a luxury property or serve all the needs of a luxury buyer. Even a top producer, no matter how good.

At the end of the day, at this price level, an agent is only as good as the firm he/she is with. The company creates the program. The agent uses it.

- *Marketing priority to the high-end*

When advertising your listings, always try to favor the big ones to create the right perception among potential home sellers and attract more sellers of the same caliber. Once you list and advertise a luxury property, you will get more of the same. The phone will ring more often.

This will also help you recruit top producers who want to associate and identify with a high-end brokerage. If and when you sign them up, you put a powerful turbo in your engine.

Advertise what you need more of. Advertising is not really about who you are, it is about who you want to be, who you want to become.

- *Keep in mind that a luxury property is not necessarily the best house on the block*

Today, luxury homes are defined as such by national and international standards, not just local/regional standards.

The minimum price and the various tiers may of course differ depending on the area and the market conditions but the bar must be placed high enough to be credible.

I realize that, in some markets, a property priced under a $1 million (adjust to what you may see fit) is considered high-end, but advertising it as such will only burn your chances of being perceived as a true player at the luxury level.

In order to be credible, you cannot cut corners, devalue the integrity of the high-end marketing program by accepting a "nice" house only for the sake of pleasing the seller and/or the agent.

The house needs to "qualify," based on location, style, architecture, size, condition, and a minimum price. Respecting strict rules can only help you in the long run.

- *Is there a difference between a so-called high-end seller and a more typical seller?*

Not really, except to say that sellers of luxury properties are often quite wealthy and most wealthy people are quite smart. That's why they became wealthy.

You cannot fool them and you don't want to try. So, the agents shopping for a luxury listing better be smart as well and well prepared with persuasive arguments extracted from your high-end marketing program rather than rely on pure salesmanship.

- *Free advice*

To get everybody (agents, staff, and managers) on board with a new company high-end program and a relevant implementation marketing strategy, I highly recommend organizing workshops in every office to unveil the program and explain it again and again. You need to highlight the rules and any and all competitive advantages.

The entire team, from the CEO to the weekend receptionist must own the program, identify with the high-end and work together to guarantee success.

Chapter 20

Open Houses ABC & XYZ

There are many ways to have a fast start in the real estate business or to grow your business substantially when you are a seasoned professional, but the best one, without a doubt, spells O.P.E.N. H.O.U.S.E: Open House.

Not only is it the best way in terms of instant benefits but it is also the easiest... and it is free!

I am 100% sold on the value of open house activity. In fact, this may very well be the single most important reason why I became as successful as I have been as an agent, an office manager, a regional manager, a general manager, an executive VP, and a president/CEO.

As a brand-new agent with zero connections and lost in a market I knew nothing about, I religiously held a property open every Sunday, if not both Saturday and Sunday. A year later I had more listings and sales than anyone in my office, a flagship office in the Bay Area.

When I became a manager, I was the first professional in Northern California (in the US?) in the mid 80's to get rid of the tiny open house ads in the classified section of the newspaper and display a huge "Open House Guide" spread in the weekend editions of the *Mercury News* and the *San Francisco Chronicle*. Expensive it was but we quickly got our money's worth. We took over the market.

For reasons that defy logic and evidence, many are the real estate company leaders or office managers who question the value and the pertinence of having associates hold properties open over the weekend (or week days).

They believe that the agents' time on Saturday or Sunday is better used showing property and writing purchase contracts.

Good idea, except that in order to take potential buyers around and eventually getting them to make an offer, it is rather essential to connect with potential buyers in the first place. It takes buyers to buy real estate. That's what open houses are all about. Eureka!

A"contacts sport"

Real estate is a "contacts sport": the more buyers and sellers you come in contact with, the more opportunities you give yourself to get listings and make sales. Simple as that. You need to go to bat to have a chance to score. It is a game of numbers.

Prospecting via emails, texts, mailings, phone, or whatever is great and necessary. When done regularly and systematically, it pays dividends regularly and more and more over time. The unique beauty of open house activity is that it pays right away.

If an agent holds a property open over the weekend, chances are that visitors will stop by. Some will be genuine customers looking to buy a home. Some may be just "lookers," but keep in mind that so-called lookers are potential buyers too.

They may not realize it just yet or they may not want the agent to know, but there is always a reason why people take the time to look at open houses.

Perhaps they only want to tour a few houses to get some ideas on what to do to make their own home more appealing. Well, let me tell you that, based on experience, it's a heck of a lot easier (and often less expensive) to buy a new home that already has what makes you tick than burn lots of time and money to spice up the existing one.

"weekend spies" and "tire kickers"

I can't count how many houses I sold, during my agent's years, to so-called "weekend spies" or "tire kickers".

Out of the few or the many open house visitors an agent might expect to see, there is a fair probability that some do not already work with another agent. They are yours to win. The more properties you are holding open and the more often you do it, the more you multiply your chances of "capturing" the wandering buyers.

In a "buyers' market," when typically the supply of properties for sale exceeds the demand, it is the magic recipe for success. It is particularly beneficial to meet prospective buyers on open house because they come to you freely, unsolicited.

They meet you on their terms. The day is Sunday or Saturday, in the afternoon. They have time, they usually are in a good mood, they have a need to fulfill and they are more willing to ask questions and listen to answers. Up to the host agent to start a conversation, establish some trust and develop a relationship that may lead to a contract.

We will see in a minute an example of how you, as a manager or a training director, can coach the agents on how to start a dialogue with visitors.

Of course, open houses are not just to meet buyers. They are what we do for the sellers' benefit. For one thing, we have a professional obligation to use diligence in trying to market a property such that we produce buyers and eventually a sale. What better way to do just that than to open and showcase a home over the weekend?

If it is your listing, it is a legitimate expectation from the sellers. Remember that even though it is great to get a listing, it is only the beginning of our work: the "real" job is to get it sold, as soon as possible and for the best terms and conditions. The sellers will appreciate your time commitment over the weekend: they "pay" for it.

Capture the attention of other sellers

Perhaps that commitment to holding the house open was one of the main reasons why the Sellers chose you as the listing agent. It should be. After all, as I like to say, your ability to get a listing and then to get it sold, is predicated on your ability to reach out to potential buyers, and that's what open house is all about.

By holding a property open, you will also "capture" the attention of other sellers: today's sellers and tomorrow's sellers. If and when they are ready to put their home on the market and look for the best agent and the best office/firm to represent them, they sure will be impressed by your time commitment and your sense of purpose.

Now let's talk about maximizing traffic to the open house. You want to be noticed. It is your show. To direct a constant flow of visitors to your property, use as many directional signs and personal name riders as possible.

Unless city ordinances stand in the way, there should be a sign at every key corner. Imagine if you have an open house with 4/5 directional signs in your town and 10 or 15 of your friends from the office do the same thing with the same number of signs... Gee, the whole town, all of a sudden, turns to the color of your company brand.

That's what you want. You want to take over the streets over the weekend. You want to keep buyers and sellers to yourself.

The manager and the firm's leaders better understand and appreciate the value of your open house commitment.

Perception is reality. Regardless what your office/company market share is in relation to your main competitors, if you have twice as many open houses as the other guys, you will be seen as the leader. You have to be physical in this market and mark your territory over the weekend.

Now let's talk about what you, in management, can train your agents to do before, during and after the open house, to leverage as much as possible the precious time they invest on a Sunday afternoon.

Before

What can or should the agent do before planting the Open sign in front of the property? It would take too long to list the many ideas I gathered through the years but the following few tips stand out:

1. Be prepared. This includes many no-brainers:
   - Know your market, particularly all listings (especially comparable properties), recent sales and overall activity.
   - Verify that you have all that you may need for a successful day: purchase contract forms, listing forms, laptop or iPad, whatever smart phone you use, business cards, personal portfolio, the company institutional brochure, samples of local housing data, listing and offer forms, brochures of the house, MLS data about comparable properties...

2. Prospecting. Come early, at least 1 hour before the open house. This will give you the time to pay a visit to about five of the closest neighbors. You want to take advantage of the extra time in the neighborhood to meet, shake hands, and say a few words to people living close by.

Be sure to do your homework on these neighbors before knocking on their doors. It would help to know their names and have basic knowledge about their homes...You never know what might happen. Use a script along the following lines:

"Good afternoon Mr. & Mrs. Barnes, I am Pete Brennan with X Realty. I am holding the Millers' house across the street open between 1 and 4 and I thought you might appreciate stopping by anytime after 12:30 to preview the house at your leisure. I'll be there anyway. You probably know that they redid the kitchen entirely last year; it came out great and that in itself is worth a look," etc.

If you hold the same house open two or three times and make a habit of calling on five or so neighbors each time, pretty soon you are going to be well known and respected as the local hero working hard as a Realtor for the benefit of his/her clients.

Another twist of the same idea is to send a few cards to neighbors a few days before the open house to invite them to stop by.

Also, when you place a directional sign on someone's front lawn, ring the bell and ask for the homeowners' permission. They will appreciate, remember your courtesy, and might reward you for it in the future with a new listing.

During

You all know to dress up the property for the part on Sunday afternoon: letting light and fresh air into the house, removing the clutter, and bringing those terrific cookies that smell so good. You have set the stage, now you have to welcome visitors. What do you do?

- Place a "Guest Book" in a conspicuous place, as close to the front door as possible. The data you need includes the email address, which is not only precious for your sake but essential to report useful information to the sellers regarding the activity.

Visitors need to jot down their information. This is not necessarily done spontaneously. Often, they need to be reminded, in a nice yet assertive way. You don't want to be obnoxious with people (who may become clients), but you don't want to ignore this responsibility either. "Sir, I would be grateful if you would write down your information on the guest book, as the sellers require it. Thank you so much."

- We all know that the most difficult thing to do on open house is to get people to open up and, hopefully, get into a real estate conversation. Something like "Hi, I am Joe Green, how are you doing" does not cut it, and "Where are you people from?" is not exactly original and inspiring. You need to be different, interesting, and pertinent. The company or the individual office should have and provide the agents with the right documents (brochures, market stats and trends, financing data, etc.) to get people to open up, ask real estate related questions, and listen with interest to what you have to say; in other words to help the agent develop a relationship.

For example, you can display market data which suggest that the market is ripe now to move-up or to invest.

After

When you have a good feeling about some visitors and learned in the conversation that they have a house to sell and wish to move their equity over to the next one, you need to seize the moment and set up the next step right away. If you wait until the next day or so to renew the contact, chances are it is already too late, the emotions are gone, and the needs are no longer pressing.

When it is too late, it is too late. So, when you are still at the open house and in a conversation with John & Mary, you need to create urgency.

It could go like this: "John, Mary, I'd like to help you with your dilemma since you have your home to sell...I tell you what, when I close the house at 5, I need about half an hour to fill out an activity report for my sellers; once it is done, somewhere around 6, I will make a point of stopping by your home, take a quick look and give you some idea as to what you could expect to sell it for in this market...Is 6pm OK or would 6:30 be better?... What is your street address again?"...

Does this sound like a good opportunity to not only sell a house but also get a listing?

Time is of the essence in the real estate business, no matter what you do. Let time work for you and create or revive the emotions from buyers and sellers that you are in the business to satisfy.

This business is not that difficult: doing the right thing at the right time and in the right place is the magic recipe for success.

That's the opportunity an open house can create. Up to management to believe in the activity and promote it with conviction.

Chapter 21

Office Sales Meetings

Among the myriad of sales driven activities that give a real estate office its character and define its strategy, I would argue that the most important is the weekly sales meeting.

It is a team building event. All members of the team are concerned and should attend:

- The associates
- The administrative staff
- The ancillary services representatives
- The manager

What a manager or a company top executive needs to accomplish in the sales meeting

Rally everyone around the office objectives and action plan and "sell" the vision of the company. It is the best opportunity to move everyone in the same direction and prepare them to fight for a common purpose.

It is the time to create and preserve a positive attitude and a winning spirit in the office,

The time to regularly reinforce everyone's commitment to action/activities,

The time to strengthen the associates' loyalty to the company and their adherence to its policies and procedures,

The time to listen to new ideas and questions,

The time to offer suggestions or solutions to recurring issues,

The time to recognize outstanding individuals and remarkable achievements,

The time to LEAD. This represents the most important time and venue for a manager to express his/her leadership, to inspire the entire office and drive it, as a single unit, to the business destination where ideally you would like it to go.

Is the word "sales" important in "Office Sales Meeting"?

You bet. It is essential. The real estate business is about sales. That is indeed what it's all about. That's the bottom line. Knowledge, experience, reputation, and activities are, of course, very important as contributing factors but only to the extent that they result in sales and revenues.

How often should the office sales meeting happen?

Every week is best, as it allows the manager to keep the team mobilized, informed, motivated, united, and focused on specific timely tasks. It should be a welcome opportunity for all concerned to start the week together.

The regular schedule is critical. If you, as a manager, decide to skip one office meeting for no good reason or suddenly change the schedule to every other week or once a month, you dilute the importance of the meeting. This may very well result in a lack of interest and soon after a lack of attendance from the associates.

Not to mention that if the company introduces new programs, or tools, or policies, and you do not have a chance to communicate the changes to the entire team in a timely fashion at the weekly meeting, it is difficult to play catch up.

You may create a disconnect between the company and the associates which, in turn, is likely to produce disinterest, complacency, mistrust and other negative outcomes.

Best day to hold the meeting

If part of the idea is to start the week together as a group, the best day is Monday, the day when the new week starts. This is particularly pertinent in the real estate business as much of what the agents do to create and handle sales happens over the weekend. They can't wait to report the good news to their friends on Monday morning.

From experience, I can attest that offices which hold their sales meeting on Monday are generally more productive and successful, as agents may otherwise "call it a day" and consequently "lose" a critical day. Not every agent works seven days a week but most agents welcome the opportunity.

It is not advisable to hold the office sales meeting the day when the local association organizes the local MLS tour of all new listings. Agents can only do one thing at a time.

In terms of time, I recommend the sales meeting starts around 8:30am or so. This should allow plenty of time for the agents to visit the new local in-house listings (including those of other offices from the same brand) once the meeting is over.

How long should the meeting last?

An hour is good. If the meeting is too short, the agents and other attendees may question why they should attend in the first place. If it is too long, many may leave before the end, which would defeat the purpose of the meeting.

Just as important is to start the meeting promptly on time. Not before and not after the announced time. Starting late will only encourage agents to come later and later and eventually not at all. Not a good idea. It is "their" meeting after all, not just "yours" as a manager. The least you and they can do is to be there and ready when the alarm rings.

All good managers prepare an agenda for the sales meeting with a clear starting time and a schedule of topics to be discussed. The agenda could be passed around at the event or preferably ahead of time. Best to email it the day before so agents and other attendees have a chance to familiarize themselves with the contents, collect their thoughts and prepare questions or remarks.

List of possible meeting topics

The key to a good and productive office sales meeting is of course to make it informative, interesting, participative and pertinent. There are hundreds of possible topics. Aside from the recurrent ones (new business and activities), the topics to be covered are chosen in accordance with timely needs and opportunities.

The following subjects are the most common (not in any particular order):

- Welcome
- New recruits
- New listings
- New sales
- Closed sales
- Open houses
- Price reductions
- Tour of new listings and properties to appraise
- Buyers and sellers' needs
- Market pulse
- Financing update
- Ancillary services update (mortgage, insurance…)
- Update on company programs
- Update on training schedule/classes
- Legal updates
- Updates from the administrative assistant, IT and marketing coordinators
- Office and company upcoming meetings/events
- Upcoming workshops and roundtable meetings in the office on pre-established topics
- Market share stats
- Tracking of office goals (month and year)
- One-on-one business plans/review meetings
- New ideas and brainstorming session
- Sales contests

- Success stories
- Theme of the week or guest speaker
- Recognition for top producers, excellence awards, and outstanding achievements (Nothing better than recognition to close the sales meeting on a positive note)
- Thank you and... go hunting!

Keys: beginning of the meeting, the end, and the theme of the week

As we said earlier, the office sales meeting should be informative and interesting but it should also be fun. It has to be an anticipated exciting event that fosters optimism, dynamism, and a can-do attitude.

With this in mind, a smart manager will never address, in front of all, personal issues and nagging administrative or technical problems. Such subjects can be discussed separately or presented by the administrative assistant or IT/marketing coordinator.

The meeting should start with a smile. There is always something great to celebrate. It should also end with a smile, to refill everyone with energy and enthusiasm. Recognition is a beautiful way to close a meeting.

In between the beginning and the end, it is important to pay particular attention to the main dish on the menu: the "theme of the week."

The manager needs to carefully prepare for the chosen topic and, whenever pertinent, invite the associates to prepare for it as well by jotting down notes on a piece of paper.

The theme of the week can be combined with the brainstorming session and can also be covered by a guest speaker.

Value and risks of brainstorming

It is essential to allow time for the agents' input. They often know as much as managers do on business matters. They are also "part owners" of the office projects and objectives.

While their feedback can be precious, it can also be dangerous. The manager needs to keep control of the discussion, not merely be part of it. Beware of hazardous topics and comments from negative people; they can easily derail the meaningful purpose of the discussion.

Guest speakers – Pros & cons

It is a good idea to occasionally invite a guest speaker, but only so long that:

- The guest is a recognized authority in the field to be covered
- The subject is important enough to justify a specialist/ expert
- The presentation has been prescreened by the manager as to avoid wasted time or embarrassing comments
- The guest comes prepared with appropriate documents for distribution
- The speaker respects the time allocated for the presentation

One of the associates, or a staff person, or a company top executive can serve as occasional guest speakers. In fact, it is a great idea to leverage them, use their particular skills to positively influence the agents.

One caution for the manager: no matter who the guest speaker is, don't let him/her take over the meeting and steal the show. It is your meeting. You need to orchestrate the entire event and be in charge.

Typical menu of the office sales meeting

- Welcome new team members
- If appropriate, welcome a guest who will speak later in the program
- Open houses report/feedback
- New listings and price reductions

- New sales and closed sales
- Buyers and sellers' needs
- Success stories
- Theme of the week or brainstorming session
- Weekly updates from administrative assistant and/or IT/ marketing coordinators
- Mortgage update
- Potpourri of company/market/business news, with documents for distribution
- Recognition/Awards
- Written list of office/company properties on office/ network tour
- Thank you, good bye and may the Force be with you all week!

Chapter 22

Strategic Meetings

Back in the day (many decades ago), I have been told that managers' business meetings created a lot of positive anticipation. Not necessarily for the right reasons. Participants (members of the select club of invitees) were looking forward to the opportunity to mingle, have a good time "away from work," and try to impress the boss.

Not so much today.

In a business world where time is money and productivity is the fuel of growth, meetings have lost much of their past luster. Today, reluctant participants are less motivated to drive to the event. They are not looking forward to another meeting long in hours and short on excitement. Some apprehend getting bored or perhaps criticized.

Are managers' meetings, where people sit around a table or face a screen, really necessary? Depends. Depends how often, how long, and what's on the menu. Show me the beef.

Generally speaking, it is reasonable to think that if the meeting agenda can easily be covered via skype or in a group phone call, it should be. Burning hours driving back and forth too frequently (more than once a month) and for no significant advantage over the phone or skype alternative, is not a good use of people's time... Unless of course a succulent lunch or breakfast is being served! (That's the facetious French side of me coming back at the smell of food). ☺

What for? Who for?

We should all agree that a meeting, any meeting, has to serve a purpose and target a clearly defined audience.

In a separate chapter, we have identified the mission of the weekly office meeting. We know what it is meant to accomplish, for both the manager and the agents.

Is the mission just as clear for a company managers' meeting? It better be. If you freeze the schedule of all the managers half a day or more every month or so, it has got to be worth everybody's time. The agenda may suggest it is, the communication may be another story.

A managers' meeting is about both information and action. Information is shared and serves as a basis for action items to be executed throughout the company's network of offices.

The same headline topics are regularly on the agenda, together with others which are time sensitive.

For instance, the meeting could cover such topics as:

- Review notable accomplishments and financial results
- Announce new programs, tools, services or policies
- Set goals and objectives
- Recruiting/retention numbers
- Recognize outstanding performances
- Sound the alarm regarding imminent or potential threats
- Listen to an outside speaker
- Ancillary services update
- Training exercise
- Marketing campaign

The list can go on and on. Worthwhile discussion topics are not hard to find in a competitive and fast moving industry like ours.

As alluded to earlier, a managers' meeting needs to have more than a rich agenda to be useful and hopefully successful. It needs to be participative. Individual managers must be given time to talk about their market challenges, present their thoughts and ideas and offer some feedback on discussion points.

Too often, a managers' meeting format is a classroom-type

setting where pupils keep quiet and listen to the teacher/CEO, or whoever.

Strategy meeting

Active participation is even more essential for an executive meeting or strategy meeting, where only the top leaders are around the table to brainstorm about the most consequential choices a company can make going forward.

Each participant needs to express his/her point of view and all the arguments that can support it. When all leaders are done with their presentations, pros and cons can be further debated. A consensus can be reached but, ultimately, the decision is left with the chief.

Implementation of any important decision should also be discussed. When can we break the news to the managers? Next managers' meeting? When and how can they relay the information to the agents? Do we need a PR piece from Marketing?

Such a meeting should also happen once a month. Ideally, it should be scheduled a week or so before the managers meeting as the decisions made at the top level will likely be part of the meeting agenda.

The two biggies

Of all the meetings that a company can organize through the year, two easily stand out:

- The "New Year Extravaganza" company meeting, scheduled within the first two months of the new year, once all numbers are finalized and the market activity is quickly warming up.
- The "State of the Union" office meeting (for each office) scheduled mid-January, once all agents are back from a possible vacation, had ample time to digest holiday meals and are now ready if not anxious to make money.

Both are huge in terms of importance. Both cover the past and the future, achievements and objectives. Both are recognition heavy. Both are meant to bring people together to show size and strength. Both are meant to create enthusiasm, pride, motivation, energy and mobilize the team members for the next twelve months, for another exciting and successful marathon.

The New Year extravaganza

No meeting is more critical than the "New Year" company meeting. No other meeting comes close. It has got to be a win. Period. It is the meeting which is going to set the tone for the whole year.

The word "meeting" is somewhat inadequate to describe the reunion of all the soldiers, managers, and generals under the same roof and on the same day. It's more than a meeting, it is the company's convention. It's a celebration. It's happiness. It's showbiz.

Music is blasting, rotating lights are flashing in bright colors, drinks are served to people as they arrive, dressed up to impress; managers and the top executives seem to dance around the room to shake hands, smile and say a few good welcoming words.

Welcome to the company once a year extravaganza.

Preparation is paramount. It takes months, if not the entire year to plan. When that phase is properly finetuned, the execution is sure to be good. Practice makes perfect.

The menu of speeches and festivities varies greatly depending on the type of organization and the style of the CEO.

Some companies are short on speeches/presentations and heavy on entertainment, like singers, dancers, sport celebrities, acrobats, clowns, illusionists, motivational gurus, from any and all disciplines, etc.

Too much is too much; too little is probably too little. Like in most things in life, a happy compromise may be just right.

The main theme of the event is "happy and strong together." The agenda must reflect the theme. Speeches cannot be avoided.

They are necessary, but they should be short, positive and energizing. It is not the time and place to dissect the previous year achievements with lots numbers and graphics all over the screens. Keep it simple and friendly.

The first word coming out of the CEO's mouth should be "Thank you," thank you for an amazing year... What You/We have done, together, is.....

Office managers as well as department managers should be recognized and some could be called on stage to present prizes/gifts and/or introduce who or what comes next.

Two segments should steal the "serious" part of the show:

- Recognition of outstanding achievements and especially exceptional top producers (sales, listings, volume, etc.).
- Charity work/contributions. We are not just about sales and money. We are community oriented. We care. We give. It is who we are.

The recognition part of the event should easily consume about half the time of the event. The winners want to be called winners. They are the examples to follow. All other agents in the room can picture themselves on stage next year. The fever can be felt around the room.

Who, when, and where

The last aspect of the celebration to consider is the time of day.

That, also, can vary greatly. In part because of space availability if the event takes place in a hotel, but mostly because of what the leader decides.

The answer may depend on whether or not spouses or significant others are invited. If they are, the choice is slim: it has to be in the evening, preferably on a weekday. In this case, dinner will probably need to be served in some fashion and dancing may be part of the program. The tab is going to be harder to swallow. Might be worth it.

My choice though, throughout my career, has always been to

hold this event in the morning, say from 8 or so to 1pm, and keep it in between the company players.

All of them have worked pretty hard all year to make the company what it is. It is their time to celebrate together, without the distraction that inevitably may result from inviting family or friends. Keep the focus on the company.

A welcome breakfast will be there when everybody arrives and a light networking lunch is proposed before good bye time. In between the two, the main course is the show.

Office "State of the Union" meeting

Much of what we said regarding the New Year company meeting applies here as well. This meeting is THE meeting of the year for the office, the most critically important. It must be your best as a manager/leader, one that will keep agents and staff motivated and mobilized till the next one, a year away. Prepare, prepare, prepare. Be ready.

It is the time to say thank you, celebrate special achievements and the special people who shined all year and gave the office the power and prestige that made it a marketplace leader, in one category or another.

This meeting is the first meeting of the year. Even if there is room in early January for a regular weekly meeting, don't even think about it. You need to start the year with a big bang. You need to start the year at full speed to create plenty of momentum. Here is the opportunity, the occasion. Don't squander it.

Just like in the case of the extravaganza meeting, the office "state of the union" will set the tone and the direction for the next twelve months. Time to dream out loud. Time to rally the troops around lofty goals and march in unison towards reaching new milestones. Time to raise pride and expectations.

There is no room in the meeting for regrets, complaints, and acrimony. Stay positive and focused on good news. OK to laugh and smiles are not optional.

Remember, this meeting is your show. No distractions. Don't invite outside guests. Keep it in the family.

It is a festive occasion. Dress the office accordingly. Balloons? Flowers? Photos of all the associates and staff? Bring plenty of goodies to bite on or have a catered breakfast delivered earlier. No alcohol, sorry.

Contrary to the company extravaganza, it is not only OK to mention numbers at the office state of the union, it is essential. Not financial numbers, just production numbers. The good ones. Those which can serve as a reference to set the bar even higher for the new year.

Here is a skinny possible agenda for the meeting:

- Happy welcoming words, including a big Thank You from the heart
- Reflect with pride on the most remarkable milestones your office and the company accomplished in the year that just ended
- Short "purified" recap of the most notable production numbers the office put on the books
- Success stories
- Market pulse: market conditions and what to expect in the way of supply and demand, economic conjuncture, cost of mortgage money, market share, etc.
- Identity, image, attitude, self-promotion/advertising
- Competitive advantages to leverage
- Business planning
- RECOGNITION: the main dish on the day's menu. Call on winners, in all categories (production, team spirit, charity, community service, etc.) to stand right next to you to get an accolade and perhaps a special prize/present. Photo time. Let's hear the applauds and the music.
- Thank you again, each and every one of you, for your accomplishments and your friendship. Thank you for a

tremendous year.
* Take your mark for the new year...
* READY? SET? GO!!!

Author Biography

The itinerary of a French journalist / American real estate icon
... Or the eternal search for business excellence

Alain Pinel entered professional life in 1965 as a political writer for the French daily newspaper *"L'Aurore,"* covering such topics as Congress and the Prime Minister.

Over the next six years, Alain Pinel wrote for several newspapers and magazines or commented the news on the radio, i.e.:

- *"France Soir"* (largest French newspaper then) - European Common Market.
- *"Nouvel Observateur"* (weekly magazine) - Western and Eastern Europe.
- *"L'Ouest Industriel"* (monthly economic/business magazine) - Editor-in-Chief.
- *"R.T.L."* (largest European radio broadcasting)

In 1972, Alain Pinel's life took another direction. Together with his wife and a one-year old son, Alain sailed to a new adventure and a new career in California.

In his new country, he successively became Regional Manager for *La Salle Extension University* in Northern California and Western Zone Manager for *U.S Industries/Beacon*, before settling in a business arena where his name soon became well known: Real Estate.

Alain started his real estate career in 1976 with *Fox & Carskadon Realtors*, in Los Altos, California. Three years later, he became the Managing Broker of the new Saratoga office, in the heart of the Silicon Valley.

In 1984, Alain was made Senior Vice President in charge of the South Bay region and a year later, became the Executive Vice President and General Sales Manager of the company.

Over his five year tenure in such a position, *Fox & Carskadon* tripled its volume of sales (to $3 billion) and emerged as one of the top residential firms in the country.

In 1990, Alain Pinel left *Fox & Carskadon/Better Homes & Gardens* and founded a new company by his name: *Alain Pinel Realtors*, using international marketing and state-of-the art technology to identify and grow with the booming Silicon Valley.

After having established *Alain Pinel Realtors* on the path of an ambitious business plan, Alain left the company with his two partners and decided to live another dream: International Real Estate.

In 1991, Alain returned to France and took the position of Sales & Marketing Director for *Sofap Helvim*, one of the leading development firms in France.

He then became Sales & Marketing Director for *Sefimeg*, then the largest investment firm traded on the French stock exchange, specializing in the buying and selling of large office/industrial/apartment buildings.

The American love affair resumed in 1995. *Coldwell Banker* brought Alain back to California as Senior Vice President to manage the West Bay region, subsequent to the acquisition of *Fox & Carskadon Realtors*.

In 2000, Alain's region, comprised of San Francisco, the Peninsula and the Silicon Valley, was the leading region in the country with an annual sales volume of nearly $13 billion and about 14,000 homes sold.

In July of 2002, well on the way to another record-breaking year, Alain returned to Europe and settled in the South of France to pursue other interests with his wife Corinne.

Leisurely life on the Riviera was not meant to last very long. Shortly after his arrival, Alain, together with three partners, founded *Imminence*, a start-up which soon changed the way real estate is done in France and part of Europe.

With a core business built around a comprehensive adaptation of the American MLS system of brokers' cooperation. *Imminence* quickly expanded to provide a complete menu of services to the industry, from marketing, financial, productivity, and planning tools to training and educational programs.

In Winter 2007, Alain spent a few days in Massachusetts to visit his son. Little did he know then that his "vacation" would eventually lead to a new exciting chapter of his real estate career After succumbing to the charm of the coastal village of Cohasset, he and Corinne bought a pied-a-terre there and, six months later, decided to leave the Riviera to experience New England living.

Well, they liked it enough for Alain to decide to get the state broker's license and resume his real estate odyssey in the US, although this time on the East Coast.

He soon became SVP & General Manager in Massachusetts for *William Raveis*, the leading independent company in New England and the 11th largest real estate company in the US.

During Alain's tenure, *William Raveis* was voted #1 "Best Place to Work in Massachusetts" by the *Boston Business Journal* and "Best Real Estate Company in Massachusetts" four years in a row by the readers of *Banker & Tradesman*.

Over the same four years, *William Raveis* saw its Massachusetts MLS market share jump 50%.

After four years of harsh winters and lots of snow shoveling, Alain resolved to leave Massachusetts and return to "his turf", the San Francisco Bay Area.

A meeting with an old friend, Gino Blefari, was enough to convince him to join *Intero Real Estate Services* (the leading brokerage in the Silicon Valley) on Day One of 2012, as SVP, Managing Officer and General Manager of *Prestigio International*, Intero's estates division.

Over the following six years, Alain wrote a weekly online blog regarding all aspects of the business (marketing, financial, fiscal, luxury, etc.) which became an industry standard and a must-read for a worldwide audience.

In 2018, a year and a half after the Pinels permanently moved to their vacation home in Palm Desert, Alain said goodbye to Intero. Commuting for that long, back & forth between Southern California and the Bay Area was no fun. Besides, when you live in paradise, you might as well take the time to enjoy it for a while and relax in the pool under the sun or in the shade from the mountains and the palm trees, right?

Good time to write a book. And another.

The adventure continues ....

Note to Readers

In the previous book, "Real Estate Behind The Scenes – Games People Play," my main purpose was to help agents and managers learn how to do the right things the right way.

The book was a go-to guide of sort for Realtors to understand the best business practices, stay out of trouble and become as good professionals as they could be in order to achieve ultimate success.

This new book focuses on the methods and systems that managers of all levels should use to objectively understand where they stand in the marketplace, formulate clear/meaningful goals and business plans, measure their performance, address any threat or deficiency, maximize their success opportunities and control their own destiny.

It is my sincere hope that "Real Estate Management Strategies & Tactics" will help you drive your business to new heights.

Business Books

Business Books publishes practical guides
and insightful non-fiction for beginners and professionals.
Covering aspects from management skills, leadership and
organizational change to positive work environments, career
coaching and self-care for managers, our books are a valuable
addition to those working in the world of business.

15 Ways to Own Your Future

Take Control of Your Destiny in Business and in Life

Michael Khouri

A 15-point blueprint for creating better collaboration, enjoyment, and success in business and in life.

Paperback: 978-1-78535-300-0 ebook: 978-1-78535-301-7

The Common Excuses of the Comfortable Compromiser

Understanding Why People Oppose Your Great Idea

Matt Crossman

Comfortable compromisers block the way of anyone trying to change anything. This is your guide to their common excuses.

Paperback: 978-1-78099-595-3 ebook: 978-1-78099-596-0

The Failing Logic of Money

Duane Mullin

Money is wasteful and cruel, causes war, crime and dysfunctional feudalism. Humankind needs happiness, peace and abundance. So banish money and use technology and knowledge to rid the world of war, crime and poverty.

Paperback: 978-1-84694-259-4 ebook: 978-1-84694-888-6

Mastering the Mommy Track

Juggling Career and Kids in Uncertain Times

Erin Flynn Jay

Mastering the Mommy Track tells the stories of everyday working mothers, the challenges they have faced, and lessons learned.

Paperback: 978-1-78099-123-8 ebook: 978-1-78099-124-5

Modern Day Selling
Unlocking Your Hidden Potential
Brian Barfield
Learn how to reconnect sales associates with customers and unlock
hidden sales potential.
Paperback: 978-1-78099-457-4 ebook: 978-1-78099-458-1

**The Most Creative, Escape the Ordinary, Excel at Public
Speaking Book Ever**
All The Help You Will Ever Need in Giving a Speech
Philip Theibert
The 'everything you need to give an outstanding speech' book,
complete with original material written by a professional speech-
writer.
Paperback: 978-1-78099-672-1 ebook: 978-1-78099-673-8

Readers of ebooks can buy or view any of these bestsellers
by clicking on the live link in the title. Most titles are published
in paperback and as an ebook. Paperbacks are available in
traditional bookshops. Both print and ebook formats
are available online.
Find more titles and sign up to our readers' newsletter at
http://www.jhpbusiness-books.com/
Facebook: https://www.facebook.com/JHPNonFiction/
Twitter: @JHPNonFiction